(a) river rising

ANTHOLOGY OF WOMEN'S VOICES

WHAT LIES BENEATH • Lana Shuttleworth • *recycled polyvinyl chloride and x-ray film*

*What Lies Beneath is a wall construction created from recycled polyvinyl chloride; more specifically, safety cones and x-ray film. Inspired by M.C. Escher's lithograph titled **Three Worlds**, this work of art challenges viewers to examine not only the surface of the artwork, but also "what lies beneath" the surface. Shards of safety cones float like leaves on the water while a koi cut from x-ray film appears from its depths. **What Lies Beneath** portrays life as we see it and the world beyond what is in our vision. (RISE exhibition, Fall 2018)*

(a) river rising

ANTHOLOGY OF WOMEN'S VOICES

An anthology of literary and artistic works
celebrating the women writers and artists of
Women Writing for (a) Change Jacksonville

Volume One
RISE AND SHINE

*Edited by Jennifer Wolfe
and Nan Kavanaugh*

Hestia Press • Jacksonville, FL

(a) river rising • anthology of women's voices

Hestia Press
1301 Riverplace Boulevard, Suite 800
Jacksonville, FL 32207
www.womenwritingjacksonville.org

(a) river rising is the first publication of Hestia Press, the newly established publishing arm of Women Writing for (a) Change Jacksonville. The founders include publisher Jennifer Wolfe; managing editor Nan Kavanaugh; designer Karen Kern; and contributing editors Jenny Anderson, Dakota Boyer, Alexa Horn, Janessa Martin, Amanda Millard, Nancy Murrey-Settle, and Sharon Scholl.

Women Writing for (a) Change Jacksonville opened in Jacksonville in 2014 as an affiliate of the national group, Women Writing for (a) Change®, founded in Cincinnati by Mary Pierce Brosmer in 1991. We established our Foundation for Women Writing for (a) Change of Jacksonville, Inc., a 501(c)(3) non-profit, in 2018 to support our outreach programs, including this anthology. Our mission is to nurture and celebrate the individual voice by facilitating supportive writing circles and encouraging people to craft more conscious lives through the art of writing and the practices of community.

(a) river rising
© 2019 Women Writing for (a) Change Jacksonville

All rights reserved. No part of this book may be reproduced at any time without specific permission from the publisher.

ISBN 978-0-578-59890-1

This book is printed on sustainably forested paper and controlled sources certified by the Forest Stewardship Council®.

Dedicated to

ALL THE WOMEN, GIRLS,

AND OTHER MARGINALIZED GROUPS

WHOSE STORIES HAVE NOT BEEN

HEARD, APPRECIATED,

DOCUMENTED, OR TOLD.

RISE • Debbie Pounders • *oil on gallery-wrapped canvas*

*After a full year of painting "Portraits of Hope" for parents who had lost their children, I had many emotions to work through. I had to decompress. All the news on television was about politics and children committing suicide from bullying. I was experiencing a lot of disappointment and pain, and I needed a big canvas to pour it all out. If I could just sit in the middle of the pain and rise from it, I felt I could arrive on the other side. So I painted **Rise**, for me. She was my release. She was my levitation through the galaxy, leaving this crazy earth just for a bit to touch the stars. (RISE exhibition, Fall 2018)*

Table of Contents

1   RISE AND SHINE

Cover, 4	What Lies Beneath • Lana Shuttleworth
8	Rise • Debbie Pounders
12	Rise Up • Jenny Hagar
13	Preface
16	Mother's Magnolia • Desiree Davis
17	Acknowledgements

19   RISE

19	Susano'O • Elena Ohlander
21	Glass • Jenny Anderson
22	Summer Skin (1976) • Penny Perkins
24	Les Girls I • Joyce Gabiou
25	The Announcement • Mary Strickland
27	Boxes • Darlyn Kuhn
28-29	Underground Railroad 9 Patch • Deborah Reid
31	Into The Light • Melissa Gopp
32	Corvo Celeste • Krista Lee Weller
33	A Crow's Eye View • Karen Riley
34	Understanding The Faithful Path • Annelies Dykgraaf
35	Endure • Princess Rashid
36	Pinky Promise • Janessa Martin
38	Avnnv (Avian Envy) • Mindy Hawkins
39	Field Guide to My Daughter • Meg Rohal
40	Cultivating the Inner Garden • Becky Craig
41	Tender • Becky Bowen Craig
42-43	Diminishing Return • Marsha Glazière
44	Flower Fields • Mimi Pearce
45	The Window • Mary Kendrick Moore
46	Spin • Nick Dunkenstein
47	Celestial • Dakota Minnie Boyer
48	Olive's Fire • Amanda Millard
49	Moving Past • Nan Kavanaugh
50-51	Stories I Can Tell • Sheila Goloborotko
52	Hoop Earings • Reem Shafaki
54	More On The Way • Penny Edwards

Table of Contents

55	Wings • Cheryle Champagne
56	A Young Girl • Gina Marie Russo
58	Surrendering To Spirit • Jennifer Bothast
59	On Death and Holding • Jennifer Bothast
60	Lest We Forget • Traci Mims
61	The Lottery • Pat Geiger
62	Afterlife • Mary Atwood
63	Vanishing • Sharon Scholl
65	Rise • Hope McMath

66 CONFLUX

66-67	Study For Lady In Green • Erin Kendrick
69	Truth Is • Jennifer Wolfe
70	No Longer Silent • Jamie Galley
71	Bitter • Hope McMath
71	Keep Walking • Terri Neal
71	Dear America • Phyllis Bell-Davis
72	Alternative Facts • Jennifer Bothast
73	Lessons From History • Beth Moore
74	I Said "No" • Amy Copeland
75	Wake Up • Linda Panetta
75	Alive • Karen Knight
76	Truth • Karen Allen
77	What Love Looks Like • Summer Van Mun
77	Ode To Jim • Lisa Weatherby
78	Definitions • Tracy Ann Miller
79	Lemon Meringue Pie • Melody Jackson
79	Where I'm From • Shinnerrie Jackson
80	Grace and the Bull • Marsha Hatcher
81	Apartheid • Cathy Courtney
82	The Lie-Berry • Jennifer Thornton
82	Pebbles on a Beach • Manisha Joshi
82	Inner Child • Lena Crowe
83	Letter to a Writer • Janessa Martin
83	Writing to Change the World • Jackie Casey
83	Care of the Container • Linda Mahoney
84	Gloria Who? • Joyce Gabiou
85	Fast Girl • Lanette Frank

Table of Contents

86   SHINE

86-87	Amaterasu • Elena Ohlander
89	How the Light Comes • Shana Brodnax
90	Poppies • Bronwen Chandler
91	Matthew Dug a Hole • Jennifer Wolfe
92	Portrait of My Mother • Karen Erren
94	Deliberate (Audre Lorde) • Sylvi Herrick
95	January Child • Mary Warren
96	Anhelo • Sonja M. Álvarez
97	So Many Places • Rachel Kohl
98	Once Upon a Time • Woody Winfree
100	Tangled Up • Elaine Bergstrom
101	Westcutter Island • Sarah Shields
102	Morning Light • Bronwen Chandler
103	Artist's Day at the Beach • Marilyn Jones
104	Speak, Brave Hearts • Margete Griffin
105	Class Poem #1 • Nancy Murrey-Settle
106	Soul to Sole • Michelle Deluca
108	Mrs. Calhoun • Lisa Goodrich
108	Once Upon A Time • Susan Gibbs Natale
109	What I Need to Remember • Kelly Komatz
110	Out of Darkness • Traci Mims
111	He Thinks He Knows Me • Cynthia Butler Jackson
112	Les Girls II • Joyce Gabiou
113	Voicing Our Screams • Erica Saffer
114-115	Manifesto: The Veiled Morena • Alison Fernandez
116	Brittle • Sharon Goldman
117	Shed • Jenny Anderson
119	Let It Shine • Hope McMath
120	Free Write • Space for You to Create

(a) river rising • anthology of women's voices

RISE UP • Jenny Hagar • *steel plate, 8 feet tall*

Rise Up *is a call to action. It's about exercising our right to peaceably assemble. This image is a self-portrait, taken from an image of me at the Women's March in Washington, D.C., on January 21, 2017. On that day, together with my mother, Kathy, my sister, Lindsay and my four-year-old niece, Hudson, I marched for many things…human rights, black lives matter, women's rights, LGBTQ rights, immigrant rights, science, clean water, and the environment. It is our right and responsibility to stand up against injustice to our fellow humans and the planet Earth. Inaction is a form of action, so we must Rise Up! (RISE exhibition, Fall 2018)*

Preface

When my children were in elementary school, they not only learned to write well, but they also enjoyed a strong art program. Every year, a parent beautifully framed one piece of artwork from each child to be auctioned off at our annual gala.

These pieces seemed to shine with a special glow once they were framed—desirable not because they met a certain critical standard, but because they were presented in a way that honored their intrinsic worth as a pure form of personal expression. As a parent, I treasured those pieces, and my children's framed artwork still hangs in my home alongside the work of professional artists.

RADICAL INCLUSIVITY

The point is, each child's piece was valued and included. This was a radical act—a radical act of inclusion. That is a value we honor here at Women Writing for (a) Change Jacksonville. Which is why, after five years of creating a community of women writers and artists here in Jacksonville, we are celebrating with an act of radical inclusivity of our own: an anthology in which every one of our writers, and every artist in our shows, could participate—if they wanted to. In a world where the majority of publishing platforms are still controlled by men who, consciously or unconsciously, find ways to shut out other voices, this is a refreshing change.

This anthology is radically inclusive in another way. It also includes the voices of all kinds of women—young and old, white and people of color, mixed-race and multi-ethnic, mothers and non-mothers, experienced writers and novice ones.

RISE • Camille Guidry • *mixed media*
(New Year's Circle, January 2017)

Preface • (a) river rising

The result is a beautiful mosaic of diverse voices and experiences, a gorgeous vessel of women's words and art that is both powerful and empowering. These pieces speak to universal truths. We hope they will even inspire your writing, or your art-making, and thereby create a ripple effect in this community of more creative expression, more truth-telling, and more conscious connection.

TRUE COMMUNITIES

In our planning, we were inspired by the words of G. Lynn Nelson, who said "true communities are possible," and that it "begins in your writing, where you come together in true community with yourself, where you give yourself permission to acknowledge your pain and joy and sadness and fear, where you begin to accept and love yourself as you are, without pretense."

We challenged ourselves, asking: How can this anthology be a circle? Can we think outside the boxed set? How can we use this anthology to help build true community here in Jacksonville? We began to see this book as a kind of living document, to be read, written in, and shared with others—a book to inspire and benefit everyone. We hope people will buy multiple copies and pass them along. By sharing our stories, we hope we can create a more connected community in Jacksonville and beyond.

SHINE • Matthew Guidry • *intaglio*
(San Jose Episcopal Day School, 2006)

(A) RIVER RISING

We chose the title of this anthology for many reasons. It reflects, first of all, a sense of place. Jacksonville's dominant feature, and perhaps its greatest asset, is water, including the river that runs through it and the sea along its border.

Preface • (a) river rising

Symbolically, water is feminine; it is generative, it is life. It is also everywhere, flowing through every part of our city and our planet. We hope the words and art of this anthology, composed by local women, will infuse our city and our world with more kindness, more compassion, and more inclusion. We hope we will collectively RISE and SHINE.

Because the water *is* rising. We are in a climate crisis, and all the waters are rising. Women's voices, too, are rising. What lies beneath the surface, as our cover art asks us? What new understandings and perspectives will help us evolve as a culture and as a community?

We hope this anthology shines some light on what we need to learn and do. Providing this platform for stories that have historically remained in the depths is an act of resistance, a cry to be heard, and a testament to the waves of change we can create when we tell the truth about our lives.

—Jennifer Wolfe, Executive Director,
Women Writing for (a) Change Jacksonville

(a) river rising • anthology of women's voices

MOTHER'S MAGNOLIA • Desiree Davis • *fabric art*

Mother's Magnolia honors my mother, who passed away recently. The magnolia tree has deep significance for me personally, representing a sense of home. Here it represents my mother as a tree of life, since she is where my life began and she was my original home, both literally and figuratively. This piece is one in a series of fabric family trees honoring various family members. I see my mother's "light" in me always—in my physical appearance, how I speak, and how I think. (SHINE exhibition, Spring 2019)

Acknowledgements

I am grateful to the many people who have helped to birth this anthology, including managing editor Nan Kavanaugh; designer Karen Kern; contributing editors Jenny Anderson, Dakota Boyer, Alexa Horn, Janessa Martin, Amanda Millard, Nancy Murrey-Settle, and Sharon Scholl; and proofreaders Kate Hallock and Michelle Busby. I also deeply thank Board members Deborah Reid, Janessa Martin, Karen Erren, Meg Rohal, and faculty members Karen Allen, Shana Brodnax, and Marilyn Jones, for their dedication to our mission.

Special thanks to Lana Shuttleworth for permission to use her work, *What Lies Beneath*, as our cover art; Foster Barnes for design consulting; Jared Rypkema for publishing guidance; Lena Crowe for copy management; and Krista Lee Weller for filming and producing our fundraising video.

Heartfelt thanks to all the writers and artists who contributed their work to this first annual anthology, a beautiful selection of the diverse voices and perspectives we've heard over the past five years of fulfilling our mission here in Jacksonville. I am grateful to them for trusting me with their words and art. I am also grateful to our donors and community members for their generosity and support.

To honor the mother-line, I thank Women Writing for (a) Change founder Mary Pierce Brosmer and my mentors in that community: Diane Debevec, Beth Lodge-Rigal, and Mary Wood-Constable. I am also grateful to mentors Kathleen Adams, Leia Francisco, and Mary Reynolds Thompson from the journaling community. I honor, too, the women who published *Kalliope*, a journal of literature and art, in Jacksonville from 1979 to 2008. We are continuing their legacy, which is carefully archived at Florida State Community College.

Many community partners have helped us do this work, but especially Donna Orender of Generation W; Teresa Miles, Lisé Everly, Shirley Webb, Sharón Simmons, and Bobbi de Córdova-Hanks of the Women's Center of Jacksonville; Sheila Spivey of the UNF Women's Center; Steffanie Fletcher of Hope at Hand; Kristin Keen of Rethreaded; Darlyn Kuhn of the JaxByJax Literary Arts Festival; Chris Boder of Ancient City Poets; Hope McMath of Yellow House; Barbara Colaciello of Bab's Lab; Basma Alawee of the Florida Immigrant Coalition; Chrys Yates of Mayo Clinic; Jennifer Jones-Murray; Cookie Davis; Lynn Harlin Skapyak; Jacksonville Public Library; the Unitarian Universalist Church of Jacksonville; Riverside Avondale Preservation Society, and many others. Thank you to all! We especially thank attorney Stacy B. Thomas of Holland & Knight, who established our foundation for us *pro bono*.

Finally, I thank my family: my mother, Dolores Wolfe, an outlier who saw the need for this work years ago; my father, Robert Wolfe, who sets the example for me in so many ways; my sisters, Ruth Anne and Liz Wolfe, who have provided innumerable hours of guidance and support; all my in-laws but especially my mother-in-law, Dianne Guidry, who helped me turn my home into a beautiful space; and my children, Camille and Matthew Guidry. I do this to honor them. —J.W.

SUSANO'O • Elena Ohlander • *acrylic and archival ink on birchwood*

***Susano'o** is the goddess of the Sea and Storms, and sister to Amaterasu (Goddess of the Sun) and Tsukuyomi (Goddess of the Moon). **Susano'o** has a Moon-esque feel with the orb she sits upon, a condensed representation of the chaos that comes with the sea and storms. She wears two masks (as she is two gods in one) and has horns atop her head. (RISE exhibition, Fall 2018)*

RISE

GLASS
Jenny Anderson

For decades, I tumble
and bump through
seabed's bristled
traps and peep
holes. Immune
to anemone stings
and sharp-
toothed things—
I ride the rip
tides.

Each bounce, break
and shift softens the
sharpness of
me. The edges
that cut
my way
through manic
currents and
tangled mermaid
hair.

I suspect when you
found me,
thumb-luscious, pocket-
smooth,
you never even
knew my
softness grew
from violent,
broken
places.

Display me now—
pile high—
with my fellow
salty soldiers.
We've all been spit
out. Purged
from Sea's belly. The
near casualties
of a war that made
us each

worth salvaging.

SUMMER SKIN (1976)
Penny Perkins

When I was in third grade, my parents moved us from northern Illinois to a little town downstate near the crossroads of interstates 70 and 57. My father had lost his job and they wanted to be closer to their parents, especially my maternal grandparents, who lived about 20 miles away from the small town we settled in.

We went to Grandpa Strawberry and Grandma Dorothy's farm every Sunday afternoon for dinner. (In those parts, lunch was called dinner, and dinner was called supper.) One summer Sunday, after the midday meal, all the men gathered in the garage.

I asked my grandma what they were doing out there.

"You don't want to know," Grandma said.

I asked my mom the same thing, and she answered just like Grandma: "You don't want to know."

I couldn't help it. I was curious. I did want to know.

My mom and Grandma were washing and drying dishes. The two of them, together, were at the sink in front of the big window that looked out over the porch and into the front yard and down the long driveway to the country road that Grandma and Grandpa's farmhouse was on. Grandma on the left doing the dipping and the scrubbing in the sudsy sink. My mom, on the right, rinsing the suds and then the drying with a dish towel when the rack got full, and she needed to make more room.

They had their backs to me. They didn't turn around to answer my questions.

"Go play with your sister," Grandma said.

"Help us with the dishes," Mom said.

Both of these options sounded equally terrible. Without really thinking about it or even planning it, I ran out the front door, letting it slam behind me. I heard my mom and Grandma both call out to me through the open window, "Come back!"

Too late. I bounded down the sidewalk from the house to the garage. It was a separate building about 20 feet from the house. It took me all of about a second to get there.

The garage door was up and open. All the men who had been hunting that morning were in the garage: Grandpa, Uncle Mickey, Cousin Mike, my father.

None of them looked at me. None of them acknowledged that I was there. None of them cared that, against the wildest of odds, I had suddenly appeared.

They were still wearing their hunting clothes and boots, squatting in a semi-circle around the carcass of a deer.

A doe. A deer. A female deer.

She was dead. Lifeless. Sprawled. On her side. The two front legs still tied together, but the back two were not, and angled out, splayed.

> *They had their backs to me. They didn't turn around to answer my questions.*

All of the men had their focus on Grandpa.

They were very intense. And acting strange.

Weird.

No one was talking.

Summer Skin • Penny Perkins

Grandpa had a hunting knife and was making a cut at the base of the deer's neck, near the shoulder. He sawed the knife back and forth, and started to rip the skin and fur away from the muscle, the flesh.

My father scooted over on his haunches toward the deer and Grandpa. He was holding a crowbar. I hadn't noticed it before. He leaned over where Grandpa had made the cut and he inserted the hook end of the crowbar under the flap of skin that Grandpa made with the knife. Then he stood up and pulled the crowbar to him with a strong tug and the skin of the deer ripped away from what used to be her body.

The sound. The sickly sound of the crowbar ripping the doe's skin away from her muscle.

I ran back to the kitchen.

My mother and grandmother just looked at me. They didn't say anything. I wouldn't have answered them anyway if they had. In the end, no one said anything about anything.

Later, I learned the word for all this savagery: venison.

PROMPT

When were the people in your life silent about something that horrified you, and how did this help shape your moral views?

LES GIRLS I • Joyce Gabiou • *mixed media*

Les Girls I is one of a pair of mixed media collages that are part of my Feminine Mystique series, an ongoing collection dedicated to all women. As an intuitive collage artist, I began by gathering black and white papers and images, then followed my intuition. *(The Art of Memoir exhibition, Fall 2017)*

THE ANNOUNCEMENT
Mary Strickland

In the winter of 1965, my father gathered us together to make an announcement. There were five of us kids, brothers and sisters, ages cascading down in stair steps: 9, 8, 7, 6 and 3. We sat clustered on pillows arranged on the floor in the den.

"I have an announcement," he said, a bit hunched over and staring intently at us. Fidgeting and squirming, the littlest girl—aged three—bounced on a couch cushion. He waited; we waited. "I have an announcement. Your mother is having another baby."

He paused, surveying us. He had our attention now. We didn't know another baby was coming. Until that moment, we had no idea our mother was pregnant. She was always tired and short-tempered, always harried. None of us knew where babies came from or connected her moods to the task of being pregnant with yet another child.

My father continued, "I didn't want another baby. I didn't want so many kids. I don't know why we have so many kids." He sat back on the couch, continuing his theme.

"I only wanted two kids but there goes your mother, getting pregnant again." He seemed angry, as we absorbed this news. My sister Ann and I were the oldest; we looked at each other and nodded. We were safe—he wanted us. He said, "If it's a boy, we are going to name him Raymond, after your mother's brother." Ann and I swiveled our heads towards the sad, now unwanted three—my two brothers and younger sister. My last brother, Raymond, was born a week later.

Twenty years passed. I was newly divorced and living in Manhattan, trying to figure out where my life had gone wrong. Insistently, I told my therapist at the time that my parents would have been happy people if only we hadn't all been born. I explained that we, their children, had ruined their lives by being born. The therapist, Ellen, leaned back in her chair, puzzled. She took a breath and said, "That isn't necessarily true. Some parents do want children around."

I was skeptical and unconvinced and remain so today. That seemed impossible. Children were a burden. A nuisance. My mind cast back to the announcement.

A few years later, when I was 33, my father eagerly ushered me into his office high over Sixth Avenue in Midtown Manhattan. I had to squint against the afternoon glare, but I was excited to be singled out by him for a visit. Even though I lived in New York and he worked there, we rarely saw each other. Displayed on his desk was a framed photograph of a young blonde woman posing on the beach in a blue polka dot bikini. With a proud smile he explained that this was his girlfriend, Lee. He said he had been chasing her for almost 10 years, since he was 51 and she was 31. They had met at a party on a sailboat.

> *My sister Ann and I were the oldest; we looked at each other and nodded. We were safe — he wanted us.*

He caressed the picture saying, "See how pretty she is? She's so independent and brave. She has her own travel company, and she speaks French. And no stretch marks either!" He grinned happily. I was appalled, but his enthusiasm and the unexpected attention kept me riveted to the carpet. He was still married to my mother. He went on to say he had always had girlfriends. He had thought about leaving my mother many times, but he couldn't because you know—"You kids were born."

I flashed back to the announcement.

That same summer, my mother had planned a lavish surprise 60th birthday party for my father. I felt

The Announcement • Mary Strickland

stretched between them; intoxicated by his sudden attention, yet sad for my mother. I held the secret close even as my mother showed off the dress she planned to wear to the birthday party. The Saturday after my mother hosted the celebration of his life, my father announced he was leaving her and never coming back. They had been married 36 years.

As soon as the divorce was final, my father married Lee. My oldest brother was best man at the wedding in Florida. The rest of us heard about it later. A few weeks after his wedding, my father invited me to dinner at the New York Yacht Club. I was sullen and he was angry. He asked, "What's the big deal about divorcing your mother?"

"Dad, Mom is 60 years old," I said.

"So what? So am I."

"Dad, she's 60. You married a 40-year-old. Who is Mom going to marry?"

A quarter of a century later, my still-handsome father lay in a hospital bed in Westin, Florida, his mouth blocked by an oxygen mask. A heavy tumor strangled his diaphragm. Assembled around the hospital bed in the darkened room were my older sister Ann and I, and Lee, still lovely and devoted to my father. It was obvious he was dying, and we were stunned.

Late in the evening of his last night on earth, he gasped his farewell to Lee and then turned to me. He croaked out, "I'm sorry about all that business with your mother, but it couldn't be helped." I nodded.

As the evening drew on and he struggled for breath, I said, "You know, Dad, I was always the smart one."

My sister Ann, catching the mood, said, "You know, Dad, I was always the pretty one."

We smiled at each other. My father eased into a morphine-induced coma, and in the morning he was gone. Nobody said, "I love you" or "Goodbye." I don't remember why not.

PROMPT
When did your parents tell you something unexpected that changed your view of them?

BOXES
Darlyn Kuhn

They are dusty, endless.

Cranky and tired, I implore my husband to stop
handing down boxes from Mama's attic,
to stop insisting we clear it all out today,
to stop, to please, for the love of all that's holy, just
STOP.

He knows me; he loves me; he can see I'm over this
incessant sorting, these perpetual decisions;
to keep, toss, sell, or deliver to people she loved
the items she tenderly wrapped and kept and labeled; things
they almost invariably decline, with sad, ungrateful smiles.

He stacks the boxes in the garage and tiptoes out,
leaving me, in silent fury,
to fume as sole survivor, the responsible one
who always, always has to handle
things no one else will handle.

Interminable, these rubber-band-bound bundles of bills
paid decades ago, these monotonous bank statements sadly lacking in zeroes, this
amaranthine documentation of fourscore years of thrift store accumulation, and then
I open a box and there they lie,
gone, but not forgotten, for forty years.

I had forgotten the stripes; I knew they were sky blue
and I'd remembered the elegant piping.
And the blood; I remember the blood, so much blood,
blood that, when washed, resembled nothing worse than a splash of spilled coffee.
A whole pot of spilled coffee.

I lift Daddy's pajamas from the box.
They smell of attic-dust and time, nothing more.
As she had done, so long ago, I hug them to my chest,
wrap their ghostly arms around myself, and rock, keening in silence.
Holding her. Holding him.

(a) river rising • anthology of women's voices

MONKEY WRENCH Get your tools together.	**WAGON WHEEL** Pack your gear.	**CROSS ROADS** A safe place, often. Cleveland, Ohio.
LOG CABIN *Dig in. Stay put.* This pattern is superimposed on a tabby cabin used as slaves' quarters at the Kingsley Plantation.	**STAR MAP** The night skies were used to navigate the way out.	**FORT MOSE** Fort Mose was a free black settlement just north of St. Augustine. It was a destination for escaped slaves when Florida was under Spanish rule.
EVENING STAR Follow the stars.	**THE WITNESS OAK** The Witness Oak on Kingsley Plantation is 400 years old. It was there before slavery and after. The Tree of Life quilt pattern is shown in the bottom left corner.	**SHOO FLY** This pattern means a liaison or safe person. The dots are in the shape of a Congolese cosmogram, placed in the floorboards of the First African Baptist Church in Savannah, a stop on the Underground Railroad.

(a) river rising • anthology of women's voices

UNDERGROUND RAILROAD 9 PATCH • Deborah Reid

Chalk paint and water-based oil on canvas

I am an artist and an attorney. I am also an amateur cartographer and a lapsed quilter. When I learned that quilt patterns had been used as signals in the Underground Railroad network, I was intrigued. This information, coupled with my attraction to Fort George Island, inspired me to combine local landscapes, maps, and quilt patterns to create the **Underground Railroad 9 Patch**. (RISE exhibition, Fall 2018.)

"My hope is that by sharing my story, others will have the courage to tell theirs in full and feel less alone."

INTO THE LIGHT
Melissa Gopp

If a woman tells you a difficult story, she's likely only telling you half. She's testing the waters to see if it's safe to come all the way out.

I tell people the moment that changed everything is when I discovered my partner was having an affair. That's the shareable half. The real moment that changed everything happened ten days earlier.

On a Tuesday night, I found the emails—sent messages from my now ex-partner's address to anonymous strangers with subject lines too sensitive to reveal. He never admitted to anything. It looked bad, yes, but he said I had the story wrong.

He caught my eyes with urgency the morning after I called him out. "If you want this relationship to last, you can't tell anybody what you found." We were standing in a parking lot, him cloaked in a suit and me cinched in low-rise jeans.

Later, I printed the emails and scraps of evidence I had gathered to justify my decision to leave him. Everybody had an opinion about it, and I knew I was in danger of doubting my own memories. I needed to hold something in my hands to prove what happened had really happened. This didn't serve me well the next morning at Starbucks, when I opened my laptop to the risqué pictures I forgot to close. Mortified, I lowered the screen and made a mad dash to click the literal X that would end my indecent exposure.

As time went on, I vacillated between questioning reality and raging at my ex. When a friend gag-gifted me a Ken doll—my consolation prize for losing my real man—I staged pictures of Ken jammed in the microwave with no pants on. Then I dipped his head in the leaky toilet of my dingy apartment.

Throughout the journey that transpired from my trauma, my writing has mirrored my progress toward healing. It's helped me see the bitter parts, where I need to let go, and when I need to speak up. What needs to be told, and how, is blurry. My story has roots beyond a messy betrayal. But I've at least arrived at a place where I'm writing from scars instead of open wounds.

The best thing about pain, as articulated by author Elizabeth Gilbert, is that it allows us to walk with others through what they think they cannot bear. This is why I write, for the people who are still hurting and desperate for love. When I left my my partner with two young boys in tow, I braced myself for a life of celibacy and financial strain. I couldn't imagine ever being loved again. I was wrong.

Today, I am using my hard-earned strength and vulnerability to bring about authenticity and intimacy in my relationships with others. I woke up from the oppressive patterns of my past and made better choices that led me to a life of love and safety. Rather than furiously working to avoid another betrayal, I dared to trust myself and my ability to perceive truth. Love saved me, but not like in the storybooks of my youth. Prince Charming didn't barge into my world and whisk me off my feet. I found the courage to initiate a partnership with a person who loves me in a way I'm still learning to do for myself, and our story started by telling him mine.

My hope is that by sharing my story, others will have the courage to tell theirs in full and feel less alone. Our culture has no tolerance for victims. Instead, we experience betrayal or abuse only to question our sanity when our realities are unacknowledged or trivialized, sometimes even by our own partners. But we'll never have anything solid to kick off from until we have the courage to see and name the truth of our stories.

We can't help but see women's stories as the casualties of patriarchy come to light in today's media. Now that we see the stories, what will we do? Will we continue to sleep, will we rage, or will we kick off and rise?

(a) river rising • anthology of women's voices

CORVO CELESTE • Krista Lee Weller

acrylic, charcoal, and artist's photographs from Italy, on BFK rives paper

Corvo Celeste *is collaged using photos I took in Milan and the Cinque Terre of Italy while filming a documentary there. She is one of five crows in my "Visitation Series," created after a crow visited my garden and looked me in the eye. A few days later, three more swooped in, and a week later, an entire "murder" of crows landed in my garden and hung out for quite some time. They were EVERYWHERE, and my garden is tiny. To mark the occasion, I added a crow tattoo to my ankle. I view crows as symbols of intelligence, change, and deep mystery—something I want to carry with me everywhere.*
(BIRDS exhibition, Fall 2019)

A CROW'S EYE VIEW
Karen Riley

A 50-year-old woman with salt-and-pepper hair lies on her back, her body stretched between two countertops on an old door. She's in an old house in Manchester, New Hampshire, and she's scared shitless. But she really wants this tattoo.

Young people move back and forth in the hallway, no door separating her from them. She feels exposed. Her youngest sister, there for moral support and to ease the tension, had already decorated her legs with Irish Wolfhounds drawn in black pen. She was the one who told her about this place, where the policemen go to get their bodies inked.

They say tattoos, piercings, and clothing choices are ways for teens to leave home without leaving home. They're visible symbols of trying on and becoming self. Sometimes we have to go through these stages again, to recapture what is lost or missing. We leave home only to return again transformed by a new way of seeing or being. These transitions call for rituals, no matter what stage of life we're in.

The ink artist is large and burly, tattooed and gruff. He holds her design in his hand and gazes skeptically at where she wants it: Just under the panty leg line, on the right hip. She wants it in a location where it will only be revealed by choice—discreet and tasteful. The design is simple, outlined in black: A dancing woman, with hands outstretched, and flowing skirts that speak to her spirit.

"Let's make this bigger," he says with authority, "and put it lower."

She stands firm. He doesn't know he's dealing with a woman who has claimed her power! Her strong spirit rises from the table, filled with memories: The passages, connections, separations, rebellions and hard-fought freedoms.

Differentiation from an identical twin.
Celebration for turning fifty.
Freedom from an oppressive childhood to an empowered marriage.

Kinship to her Celtic and Nordic ancestry.
Solidarity with all those invisibles and enslaved; branded cattle and other captive spirits.

This tattoo symbolizes the spirituality of a woman with a dancing heart, one who listens deeply, and isn't afraid to travel into the inner and outer world of pain and joy. This is her act of leaving home and returning again.

She has risen and left her old self so many times.

Overruled, the artist then instructs her to pull her shorts down to her knees. She raises her body on the table to shift them down. Modesty is not an issue. The

> *She has risen and left her old self so many times.*

painful process begins and so does the swearing. She doesn't care who hears the loud "fucks!" that come flying out of her mouth like crows. They mimic the dancing tattoo, flying around the room and out the door. Before he's finished, another flock of "fucks!" flies between the laughing sisters, circling the room before exiting.

When it's all over, she breathes the slow breaths that have birthed new life in the past. The pain has always been worth it, whether it was in birth or death.

She rises and leaves. She rises and leaves to return again, claiming self yet again.

This return severs identicality. It ritualizes the healing of invisible wounds. It erases possession by others with a deliberate mark. This lying down and rising again, marked by the indelible ink, says she can return home yet again. She is transformed, again and again.

(a) river rising • anthology of women's voices

UNDERSTANDING THE FAITHFUL PATH • Annelies Dykgraaf • *clay print*

We all have our own path that we must either follow to completion or forge as a new beginning,
but it is in doing so that we learn to persevere and thrive. (SHINE exhibition, Spring 2019.)

ENDURE
Princess Simpson Rashid

Some people crack
But not me.
Not always.

My plan is to cheat the devil
whenever I can. Grow tall
instead of becoming a broken thing.

To rise after being plucked
squeezed and pinched,
slapped and counted out.

To rise after the grinding
down by time. After the sharp rocky cuts
inflicted by supposed lovers or casual friends.

My plan is to endure the struggle
of living. To rise and stand firm against
the breaking of the world.

PINKY PROMISE
Janessa Martin

I am changed. Not because I wanted to be. I would have given anything to stay just as I was, 24 years old, walking sockless in flat leather Mary Janes among the gold and rust-colored maple leaves of Virginia. Wearing long polka-dot dresses tied with belts. Walking, oh God, just walking, camera in hand. Listening to the rustle of trees, squinting across the frothy river waves, breathing in air I had never breathed in before. Crisp, succulent air. Air that moved through the second-floor house we rented on Westover Avenue. Air that made the original glass window panes rattle in their chipped white frames.

Sometimes, I would stop for a moment at the porcelain sink and look out over the houses, the neighboring park, the hospital, into the sky tinged with orange and streaks of pink. Or I would stop in the blue-carpeted sunroom, enveloped by the branches and leaves of our neighbor's tree. Or I'd stop on our stoop with the four brick stairs, sitting there, watching the passing cars and bicyclists. In these quiet moments, I held my head back in reverence. I let the air caress my neck, rub my cheek, and soothe my soul. I was content.

For a moment. For those small moments, I was content.

But I was 24 and I found myself wanting. This was not what I had dreamed: this time, this place, these people.

Because when I was 12 years old, I had made a promise. Sitting on the grand stoop of my aunt's home located at the top of Bigelow Street, sitting there next to the gold-plated mailbox, overlooking a hillside of homes. At 12 years old, I had promised to move to Boston, Massachusetts and make a life for myself.

I told no one. The dream belonged to me.

I was so young. So resolute. So connected to the dream that when met with another life opportunity, I was closed to it. Closed to the prospect that anywhere other than Boston could bring me happiness.

Because that opportunity was not my own. I had followed my husband to Norfolk, Virginia, after he had secured an engineering job with the Department of the Navy in the final months of college. He did not know that I was the first to find out. That I had opened his email and read the offer letter before even he had the chance. He did not know that I was deflated. That thoughts—scary, fearful, "this isn't right" thoughts started to race through my mind. I was so overwhelmed that I had to go for a walk outside. But when he came home and opened his email, and turned towards me with jubilation, I smiled.

And I continued to smile, day after day, month after month. Even though I was crying inside. Because this wasn't right. Virginia wasn't right.

Because, I had made a promise.

Because, I had made a promise.

And so my mind continued to scream, and when that didn't work, my body began to scream. Tension headaches left me immobilized in bed. My hands started to shake. I was rushed to the hospital, because the skin on my thighs turned to the consistency of cottage cheese. Hives, I learned.

We searched the apartment for possible contaminants and reviewed my diet, neither of us understanding at that time that it was change that was sickening me. I was allergic to unforeseen change.

Because, I had made a promise.

And, I had made Matt promise, too, that he would honor my dream. And that some day, my place would become his place, and there in Boston, we would make a life together.

. . . . .

It was during our senior year of college, when we would venture out to Buffalo Wild Wings for a weekly date night. We always sat in the back room, reserved

Pinky Promise • Janessa Martin

for those over the age of 21. That night, we sat in the middle of the long veneer bar on black, backless barstools, watching hockey. We sat close, as we always did, Matt pulling my barstool next to his, our bottoms and knees touching.

"We have to be open to all opportunities," he said. "I can't determine where I'll get a job."

"Boston has been my dream since I was a young girl," I replied. "That is where I want to go, that is where I've always envisioned myself. There and nowhere else. That's it."

He smiled, his you're-not-easy-to-please-but-I-love-you-anyway sideways smile. "Janessa, I promise I will get you to Boston."

"Pinky promise?"

He said nothing. But his eyes turned downward.

I followed them.

And there it was, waiting in the space between us, Matt's left pinky finger. I smiled and held out my right one. And like children making a playground pact, we entwined our littlest fingers and promised to go to this place, this place and nowhere else.

. . . . .

Years later, after Virginia, after my quarter-life crisis and after the birth of our first child, we did make it to Boston. We settled in a quaint New England town just north of the city.

It was a graduate scholarship to Boston University that prompted our move there. It was my intellect, my aspirations, and my indomitable will. Why younger me thought I needed a man to propel my story forward, I will never quite understand. Insecurity, maybe. Unresolved trauma, more likely. Fear, most definitely.

I was scared. I knew what I wanted, but I was afraid to go forth alone.

But I made it. We made it there together.

And Boston was magical. The city and the surrounding areas were everything I had dreamed they would be sitting atop my aunt's stoop as a little girl. I loved the walks to and fro, the trains passing by on their rusty tracks, the historic shops lined along cobblestone streets, the fall leaves sticking to the wet black pavement, and the hikes in the woods and along the sea. Such beauty.

But also such unimaginable wealth and privilege. Matt and I both knew we could love and enjoy this area but that somehow, it was closed to us, and always would be. For one thing, in grocery stores, at the library, walking around town, I was often followed by curious stares and questioned about the difference between my son's pale white skin and my caramel brown complexion.

Every place has its shadow, and Boston was no different.

That's what I wish I could have known as that young

> *Every place, everyone, everything, lives in lightness and darkness.*

girl who lived in absolutes and all-or-nothing thinking. That every place, everyone, everything, lives in lightness and darkness. In Virginia, I saw only a cage because that's what I wanted to see. In Boston, I saw only comfort because that is what I longed for.

To that young girl, the younger me, I would say, "Slow down. Breathe. Take a peek outside the tunnel and see all the gradations alive there—all the potential for circumstances, people, and places to surprise you. Be open. There is beauty everywhere, in this moment and the next and the next and the next."

(a) river rising • anthology of women's voices

AVNNV (AVIAN ENVY) • Mindy Hawkins • *gourd, fabric*

I am intrigued and inspired by two sculptural mediums: the natural and organic shape of gourds and the sculptural and textural characteristics of hand-made soft figures. The combination of these two elements sparks my imagination and inspires me to create art that tells a story. In many cases, the theme of the piece is represented by a play-on-words using iconic characters, both real and imagined. The gourds are hand-carved and dyed and the figures and their clothing are hand-sewn and sculpted. The two mediums are combined to create a harmonizing composition. (The Art of Memoir exhibition, Fall 2016)

FIELD GUIDE TO MY DAUGHTER
Meg Rohal

Jumping out of the pickup truck, my daughter, Christine, approaches the long, barbed-wire-topped gate. The roads in this remote Utah nature preserve necessitate a four-wheel drive vehicle. The narrow, rocky byway is barely passable due to large holes filled with water from the storm that had moved through the previous night. We don our hip-high waders, rain gear, and protective gloves. As Christine marches up the road, I follow slowly, fearful of falling on my backside in the thick mud.

It does not surprise me to be here. Ecology suits my child. She began to hone her skills as a toddler digging in the green turtle-shaped sandbox. The shelves of her room were stacked with the boxes of rocks and fossils of her prized collection. Now she is a Ph.D. candidate, tasked with determining the best way to control an invasive species. I'd come along on this cold, grey September morning so I might have a better understanding of the project that has consumed her life for the past four years.

We are at one of the research sites where she's field-testing various treatments to eradicate the dreaded invasive plant, the Phragmites. The Phragmites grows over six feet tall with a plume at the tip, much like a Florida sawgrass. A tuberous plant that grows in wetlands, when it invades, it chokes off all other plant life. From the path, we can see its tentacles stretching out for miles. It has become a sea of undulating stalks and leaves, wiping out the habitats of the birds and ducks that make this part of Utah home—or once did.

A prized native species of England, the dried stalks of Phragmites become the thatch for the roofs of those lovely English cottages. But in Utah, and, alarmingly, in many other parts of the United States, this weed is taking over the wetlands. The density of the plant is so thick it's impossible to pass through a field of them. Christine tells me she's actually been swimming atop the mass of plant life in order to mark her research plots.

We reach a tall metal marker that indicates the beginning of the first of her five one-acre plots. She has a total of six research sites spread across the Salt Lake Basin. Each plot received a specific treatment in the spring, and she is here to measure the effectiveness of those treatments. With a meter-wide quadrant locator made of PVC pipe, she walks into the plot, counting her steps and carefully measuring different data sets, recording the results on her covered clipboard. One, two, three, four, five sets of data; recorded at five different locations per plot, five plots at six different sites—the amount of information is staggering.

...she tramples relentlessly through the thick plants.

I watch my petite daughter, boots up to her waist, big floppy hat set cockeyed atop her long brunette hair, as she tramples relentlessly through the thick plants. At some points, it is easy to see her, the treatments having worked. At other times, I lose her: only the sound of the squeaky muck under her feet, the PVC pipe waving wildly over her head, and the faintest white of her hat visible.

I ponder the immensity of this task she has taken upon herself, the fight against the Phragmites, akin to ridding the South of Kudzu. Why take on such an impossible assignment?

Christine understands that while the battle against this plant might be difficult and quite possibly never-ending, one small discovery could make a profound difference for the environment she treasures.

My heart swells with pride. This girl. My little girl who loved to look for roly poly bugs in the yard and still thrills at finding shark's teeth on Florida's sandy beaches. Here. Fighting Mother Nature and the ravenous plant that threatens to choke the wetlands. Fighting for the birds and ducks. Never giving up.

CULTIVATING THE INNER GARDEN • Becky Bowen Craig • *paper collage*
(Art and Soul Series, Spring 2015)

TENDER
Becky Bowen Craig

The time will pass
whether we are paying
attention
or not.

We will continue
to grow,
whether we tend ourselves,
or not.

An untended garden
becomes tangled
and light cannot reach
the tender new shoots
of possibility;

The soil
unturned and hard,
closed to the vibrant energy
of rebirth and renewal.

An untended tree
can get itself
into trouble,
its branches too long
and heavy
to sustain themselves.

We are the tenders
of the gardens
and the trees
and ourselves.

Our best effort
and intention
and love
must go into
the tending.

Diminishing Return

Marsha Glazière • *acrylic/mixed media*

The law of DIMINISHING RETURN is a fundamental principle of economics, but in this painting I am "stretching" that principle to include the reality of climate change—whereby we humans, and especially industry, continue to produce more and more of everything—good and bad, needed or not.

In the case of climate change—the return is self-destruction instead of the anticipated gain of profit and/or perceived ease and comfort.

Arctic ice caps increasingly melt due to rising atmospheric temperatures, and wildfires grow in intensity. The devastation of the earth and and all life forms is impending if human behavior and corporate enterprise globally are not significantly changed or reversed—and sooner rather than later.

(SHINE exhibition, Spring 2019)

(a) river rising • anthology of women's voices

FLOWER FIELDS • Mimi Pearce • *acrylic and oil on canvas*

Art has the power to calm, transport, and heal the spirit in times of turmoil. **Flower Fields** *takes me to a ridge where I am surrounded by an abundance of fragrant Spring wildflowers. There's a light breeze. It's warm but not hot. I can see far into the distance, and all is at peace.*
(Shine exhibition, Spring 2019)

THE WINDOW
Mary Kendrick Moore

In the tiny little kitchen on George Circle, my mom, in her yellow sleeveless cotton blouse, over bright blue pedal pushers, stood at the single window over the dull white sink. Water running, she rinsed the dishes after our pimento-cheese-on-white-bread sandwich from lunch.

In that space, no larger than a four-foot square, she made enough food to feed an army. The hum of the mixer often signaled the start of a golden yellow pound cake as she watched the red cardinals out the back window.

Once a year, we would hear the crash of a hammer onto a hairy coconut that heralded the approach of Christmas, awaiting five gushy layers of coconut cake from the oven. When fresh peaches arrived from the orchard down the street, the tiny counter space was filled with flour as we rolled out dough for fried peach pie puffs—the sizzle of the fryer not far behind.

The kitchen cabinets around that window were the dullest, pale green you can imagine. A cornice board, cut by my dad, stretched across the window and a bright fluorescent light was tucked behind it. I can still smell the sawdust from the day he cut that board.

A lot happened at that kitchen window. Mom watched me like a hawk as I played with friends in the backyard. She could see the laundry she hung on the clothesline, and I think she could tell just by looking out that window when it was time to bring the laundry in.

First thing in the morning, after the smell of bacon filled the house, Mom stood at that window, looking out beyond the backyard. She could hear the great rumble of the school bus motor, like clockwork, before she could ever see it coming 'round the corner. Time to scramble then—down to the corner to catch the bus.

It was at that window I learned that not everyone is treated the same.

We could also hear the giant rumble of a different motor—the trash truck. As soon as the echo drifted into the neighborhood, she locked our screen door and closed the back door. When I looked out the window to see why, all I could see was a man with dark, brown skin walk into the backyard, clang the metal lid off the trash can, and carry it on his shoulder all the way out to the street and back. She stood at that window and watched his every step.

One day, the noisy rumble and giant motor of the

> *It was at that window I learned that not everyone is treated the same.*

trash compactor filled the house, louder than usual. But the screen door was not locked; Mom continued her dishwashing while the back door stood wide open. This time, the man who walked into the backyard was a white man.

Windows can go two ways. They open up to fresh air, and they keep in stale air. We can look out, or we can look in, sometimes straight into the deep wells that have formed our souls.

— *Memoir Series, Fall 2017*

(a) river rising • anthology of women's voices

SPIN • Nick Dunkenstein • *traditional photography*

Spin speaks about transformation from being a simple human being to something beyond the realm of realism. The dancer changes forms, from an understandable being, into a transparent distortion capable of crafting a sort of light magic. Our capabilities as mere beings can outlast our mortality. It's a magic we all possess, even though only few really tap into it. Spin speaks about transformation into a higher self. The dancer is telling you to shine in your highest plane—it doesn't matter what you look like, who you are, what you believe: Shine on, and shine bright. (SHINE exhibition, Spring 2019)

CELESTIAL *(a response)*
Dakota Minnie Boyer

You say,
"some of us do not
know how to swim.
We walk on water," but I
would like to revise that thought
and say we walk across ice
like the many before us, escaping
ancient Russia and her tundra
for the New World,
for then, she truly was.

We walked across ice
in fur-bound boots, children on our hips,
slung across our chests, some nursing
as we pull carts, carry the spear and bow,
daggers strapped to our legs.

We walked across ice
and watched it melt behind us.
Try that trick on for size, Moses.
We gazed upon the land of our past
and made our way to community—civilization,
to golden headdresses and lizard earrings.

We gave up our water priestess
for the earth, for our galaxy.
Let us collect constellations on a map,
call it home and breathe out
mathematics, science, medicine.
Let us gaze into the night and know
the shadow of Sirius against Orion.
With a child strapped to our chest,
we gave up the sea, raised our voice
cosmic,
celestial,
universal women.

—Anthology circle, Summer 2019
A response to "Water Women," by Alla Renee Bozarth

OLIVE'S FIRE
Amanda Millard

A year after adopting my baby daughter, Olive, I took her to visit my hometown and the many relatives eager to meet her. Amid the chaos, I wanted just one thing: a photo of my daughter with myself, my mother, and her mother. But I knew that creating this heirloom would mean wrangling two of the most willful women in my life: my resistant, camera-averse grandmother and my equally resistant, squirmy daughter.

Olive and her great-grandmother are not biologically related, and they have very different ethnic backgrounds and features. But when I first saw the photo, I was struck by their sameness—by the way their ferocity seemed to light them both from within. This makes them stunning in a fearsome way, and it can make loving them a fretful, exhausting job.

Yet they are biologically related, as we all are. We are all descended from a single woman, often known as Mitochondrial Eve, who lived relatively recently in human history. We can all be traced, through this unbroken mother-daughter chain, right back to her. In her day, there would have been nothing remarkable about her. But she had the luck, or perhaps the grit, or maybe the smarts, to survive in a very grim world. And she raised daughters who could survive in it, who raised more survivor-daughters.

I cannot help but imagine Eve as my grandmother, standing at that desperate moment in human history—bitching her way right through that volcanic eruption or plague or asteroid, not really caring if she ticked off the cavemen. Because that same inner fire that makes her tough to love also makes her tough.

Though Grandma has not faced near-extinction, she has faced a life that many people would not have survived. The poverty and abuse that characterized her early life made her who she is. She weathered adversity and raised her two daughters through it.

Science tells us that adversity changes not just our minds, but our very DNA. Our experiences express our genes, and we pass on this epigenetic legacy to the next generation. Women are particularly vulnerable when it comes to inheriting big challenges—depression, anxiety, and related health problems. But I also think we are the carriers of the fire that keeps people surviving through dark feelings and the world's darkest days.

Olive's fiery will may seem too large for her tiny self or for the little life she has lived thus far. But not when I consider the countless generations of struggle and hurt that have been passed on to her, flowing from mother to daughter, crashing down on her. To raise her, I can offer the burdens and joys of my own family's legacy: my great-great-grandmother's endless grief for the baby who died crossing to the New World, the instinctive midwifery skills my great-grandmother used to deliver my aunt unexpectedly, my grandmother's rape, my years-long search for a daughter to call my own, that first failed adoption of a daughter I mothered only in my heart.

> *Olive's fire gives me hope and makes me strong.*

To that, we must add a whole birth family's history—the parts we know and the bigger part that Olive's birth mother will share with her only when they're both old enough.

Finally, there is her own adversity. On her first day in this world, Olive said goodbye to her first mother and was given to a new stranger-mother. No one asked her permission. She was the most important member of this delicate, monumental family merger, and she never got a vote.

But Olive, like the women before her, is a survivor. Whether from her genes or from her family, she has inherited an old, deep power. I fear what our turbulent modern world holds for her and for all of us. It would be easy to allow this fear to consume me. But standing at this desperate moment in human history, Olive's fire gives me hope and makes me strong.

MOVING PAST
(a found poem)
Nan Kavanaugh

the literature of the sun
or the husband's narrative
is not the same as a deep bay
spilling out into the Caribbean
the round, blue space
warm in its darkness
is the expression of feminine

moving past:
the debt of the homemaker
to pursue a career
is the homeless child

moving past:
the bystander effect
of women couch surfing
this Age of Aquarius

the Age of Information, a baby
maybe a handful of months old
in that infinite black soil
of the universe
how do you plant a voice
write it

the roots are the collective struggle
community is in the creating
in this season of women's work

—Anthology Circle, Summer 2019

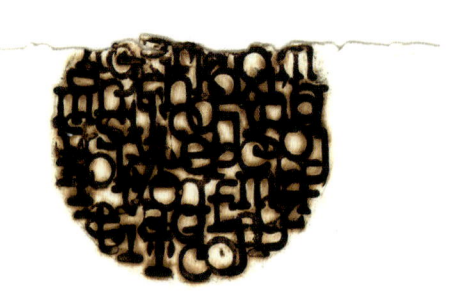

Stories I Can Tell

Sheila Goloborotko
itaglio embossment, Chine-colle, and pyrogravure

Is there still a place for a lasting image in the sea of endlessly updating news feeds?

In turbulent times, it can become overwhelming to observe the torrent of information flowing past, and all too easy to become swept up in the churning tide. Can we find pause within such an environment and create imagery that is not merely pamphletary and reactive, but portrays the contemplative moment before our responses?

This series is a visual contemplative manifesto. It was created to slow one down, and create pause from the widespread distribution of ideas challenging us in the 21st century by the scrolling social media feed.

(SHINE exhibition, Spring 2019)

(a) river rising • anthology of women's voices

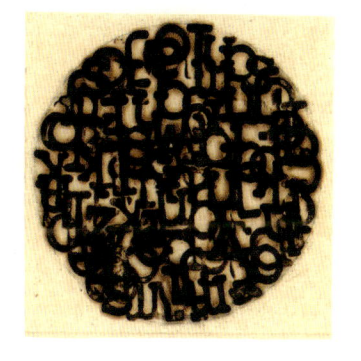

HOOP EARRINGS
Reem Shafaki

She comes to me to help her put on the big hoop earrings, the ones that match the sweater she's borrowed from her big sister.

"Sorry, I can't," I say. "I'm already a few minutes late for my 7:30 a.m. conference call."

"Is it a video call? Can you put them on for me while you're on the call?" she pleads.

"It's a video call," I say, as I rush to put on a blue hijab and smooth the bed covers in case my video camera accidentally moves half an inch to the left and shows our bed in the background.

She looks at me with her big brown eyes, disappointed, but understanding. By now, the girls are used to my sudden switches from one role to another, from nurturing mom to businesswoman, like someone suffering from a multiple personality disorder. One moment, I'm the mom packing school lunches in the kitchen and cutting apples and oranges for a quick breakfast. Then, in the blink of an eye, I'm the mom yelling, "You need to pack the rest of your snacks and fill your water bottles, I have a conference call NOW. No, sorry, I can't French braid your hair. Yes, that picture you drew is lovely, but I can't look at it right now."

"Maybe you can put my earrings on if you slide your chair all the way to the left. They won't see me," she suggests, her big eyes imploring, imagining how complete her outfit would be if she just wore those big girl earrings.

"Sorry, it won't work, plus I'm sooo late," I say as I shoo her out the room and close the door.

"Good morning! How's everyone?" I breathlessly greet the faces on my computer screen. "Yes, I'm very excited to be discussing our strategy for this year."

I hear the door close, the girls leaving for school, while one of the three men on the conference call shares how confident he is that we can reach $1.5 million in revenue this year, and how we're poised to become a $100-million company.

I hope she's not too disappointed she couldn't wear the earrings. I shouldn't have spent time putting the dirty dishes in the dishwasher and trying to tame the monster left over in the kitchen from the girls' cooking project last night. The one they conducted while I was

> ...my sudden switches from one role to another, from nurturing mom to businesswoman, like someone suffering from a multiple personality disorder.

at my writing circle. They made Pinterest-inspired breaded cheese bites in the waffle maker, plus spaghetti with pesto sauce. And yes, they cleaned the kitchen, but the monster always grows new tentacles, and is always lurking in some dark corner or other, ready to spring at the unsuspecting kitchen. I never succeed in putting him in his cage and locking him up for good.

Maybe her dad or big sister managed to put them on for her. Oh, I should have just let the monster be! He always comes back anyway, and he'll surely be back again tonight after the family has yet another dinner on their own.

Or I could have just not put my camera on right away.

"So Reem, what are your top-of-mind goals for the company, as well as for yourself personally?" says one of the men on the screen.

Hoop Earrings • Reem Shafaki

What, me? Just like that, without giving me time to prepare?

"Err, well, for the company, we need to diversify our projects and do more implementation work." But what I want to say is, "I'm sick and tired of working on stupid reports. All these numbers are not very interesting to me. Let's actually start doing something instead of just talking about it and telling others how they should do it! Also, we need to get more retainer projects, so that you can actually pay me on time, and so we can stop trying to accomplish great feats every single time, with impossible deadlines that lurk like dark clouds above our heads, threatening to pour buckets of water on us."

"What's your BHAG?" the boss asks me.

I think, My Big Hairy Audacious Goal? I don't have one! And if I did, I wouldn't be sharing it with you!

"As for my personal goals," I continue, "I learn by doing, so I'd like to learn to develop better strategy frameworks. I'm also developing my Facebook advertising skills. Oh, and I'm also taking a 'writing class,' which will be helpful for all the blogging we plan to do and all the reports we write."

A writing class. That's all they need to know. The words, "We're a circle of women spilling our deepest secrets onto paper, sharing our raw emotions in written form," is not something these three men want to hear. I can just imagine their eyes growing wide, as wide as hoop earrings dangling from a little girl's ears.

PROMPT
Finding balance in life is difficult. What are your challenges?

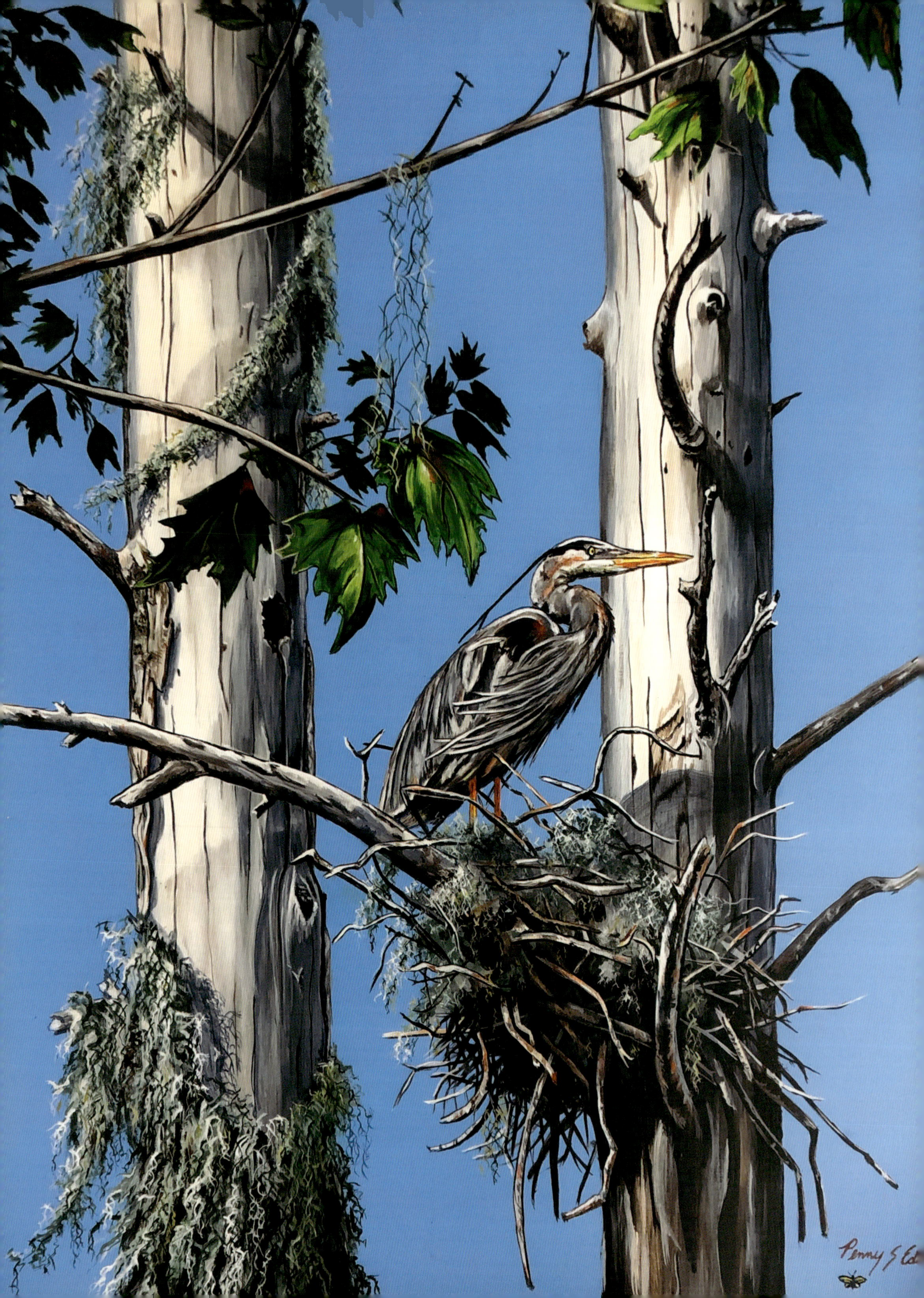

WINGS
Cheryle Champagne

The birds built a nest outside my workplace window. I watched them each day, as they wove their design in tandem, creating something delicate, sturdy, and safe.

Home.

Soon there were eggs, then babies, then busy parents dropping food into three tiny, yawning mouths—each beak adorned with yellow lipstick lacquer.

The afternoon storm came on a day when I was deep in grief, having returned to work too soon after burying my mother. I was going through the motions—still a little numb, incredulous to the fact that she was really gone.

The storm blew rain against the window, the pinging sounds reminded me of the baby birds and their mother. At the window, I found her positioned over her babies, her wings an umbrella.

On this day, in this storm, the mother bird called me back to the world. From the descent of my grief, she called me back to a new life, a life without a mother. This was not the end. This was a new chapter without a mother.

I felt my way through days and nights of grief. I learned to accept my longing for the things I missed most about my mother—the feel of her soft skin and the sound of her voice. I still miss these things after all these years. But I've kept the memory of that tiny mother bird, on that dismal stormy day, as a reminder that my mother's love will always be with me.

—Write + Hike, Spring 2019

MORE ON THE WAY • Penny Edwards • *acrylic gouache*

There is so much that is inspiring in nature when you take the time not just to look, but to see. In all of nature there is a light that shines, a soul to glimpse. In my wildlife paintings, I try to capture the soul of the animal by the expression in its eyes, and how the light brings them to life. At Circle B Bar Reserve in Lakeland, Florida, I spotted this great blue heron on its nest high in the trees. (SHINE exhibition, Spring 2019)

A YOUNG GIRL
Gina Marie Russo

A young girl, maybe seven or eight, stands beside her mother's pill drawer. She looks into a disastrous mess—pill bottles strewn about, capsules and tablets littering the base of the drawer.

She picks them up, one by one, carefully reading the letters and numbers on each one, the same way she reads the ABCs posted on the wall of her classroom at school every day. She knows this space, and she goes through the motions seamlessly. This little girl is a special one, and not just because she is me. She is an old soul; she has already lived lifetimes in her short years.

As I place each pill into its bottle, I pause for a moment each time. I know some of them by sight, but not all of them. Thank goodness for the descriptions on the labels of each one. I wouldn't be as proficient at this if it wasn't for them.

This ritual isn't anything new. It happens every few weeks or so, when I notice my mother fretting about in her drawer as she goes to take her morning (or afternoon, or evening) medication. She moves to this space without a sound, but her energy is palpable. I follow her with my eyes as she moves herself closer and closer to her spheres of sanity. Hands held to her sides, usually with a cigarette resting between her fingers, her shake is barely noticeable. I have keen eyes for the short wobble of her fingers. We've even turned it into a game, she and I. "Mom, put your hand out! Let's see the thing!" And as I place my hand next to hers—mine steady and sure, hers moving with the gentle wake of nerves that needed calming—we would laugh. Standing in the kitchen, it was our own little moment together. One of the many moments we created together, nowhere near "normal." But that was kind of our thing, anyway.

On this day, I can feel the fervor in her steps. She's late again, isn't she? She hastily pulls out each bottle, opens it with a clumsy twist as she struggles over the child lock. She pours the contents into her hands. I hear a clink...make that two...of something solid hitting the bottom of the drawer. She doesn't seem to notice; maybe she's counting, but who knows.

"Mom, how many of those?" I call from the kitchen table as I watch her.

"Two, just two of these. And one of the other." She tries so hard to assure me with her words, that she is certain, but her tone tells me otherwise. I wonder if she is taking too many or too little today.

With a brisk slam, she finally flits away from the drawer and I make my way over to it. Having watched her

> *I have keen eyes for the short wobble of her fingers.*

closely all these years, I know what I will find. I know the wreckage that lies at the bottom of that drawer. And I know that it will mean disaster if the wreckage stays in its current state.

So I carefully pick up each capsule and tablet and hold them gingerly; I slowly rotate them between my fingers. I watch the light catch on the waxy coatings of some and I feel the white, chalky residue appear on my fingers with the more powdery, circular ones. The colors of these pills amaze me. No wonder little kids confuse them for candy.

Light blue ones shaped like *Tic Tacs*.
Pink, diamond-shaped ones that look like *Chicklets*.
Plain ole chalky ones, just like a *Smartie*.

My eyes rest on the little letters and numbers etched on the sides of each one. I always wonder how they got them on there. And I always try to figure out what those letters and symbols mean. Each pill has its own unique language and personality to me. I assess each one by size, color, texture, and shape, and my mind starts asking the questions I have repeated to myself too many times before. I should know the answers by now.

A Young Girl • Gina Marie Russo

"What does this one do again? Is it the one that helps her fall asleep or the one that keeps her from sleeping all day? Maybe it's the one that stops her from crying all day. Oh! Or the one that helps her thyroid!" I hear about that last one a lot. She would always say "I don't have a thyroid anymore, so I need these pills to help me regulate my weight!" or something like that.

A voice in my mind whispers:
"What if I just threw them all down the toilet? Nothing would happen right? But wait…what would Mom say? What couldn't she do if I did that? Could she do anything at all?
What would Dad say?"

And with each question I ask myself, I come to the realization that I will NEVER know the answers to those questions.

Why?
Because I am GinaMarie, protector of the house.
I am the Good Girl.
I make Wise Choices.
I am Responsible.

And GinaMarie would Never Do That. For I know, even at seven or eight years old, that these pills are sacred. They are the pharmaceutical buoys that keep our family afloat, at least when Mom chooses to take them on time. They are our solace from the chaos. And I can tell you right now, there is no way I would be the one held responsible for unleashing that beast on the rest of my family.

In fact, in that moment, I have a brilliant idea!

"I can fix this! I am responsible! This will be my job from now on. I'll be in charge of this drawer and all the contents within it." I am very proud of my decision, if you can't tell.

I deftly pick up and replace all the remaining tablets and capsules in their bottles with greater speed and precision than normal. My adrenaline is pumping now. I want to tell her my idea. I make sure to leave the few mismatched pills at the bottom of the drawer, but tuck them away in a corner under some papers lest my little brother comes around and finds them.

I proudly survey my work and I call out, "Mom! Come here and look! I fixed the drawer! Can this be my job, now? Please?"

PROMPT
When did you take on responsibilities as a child that were not yours to take?

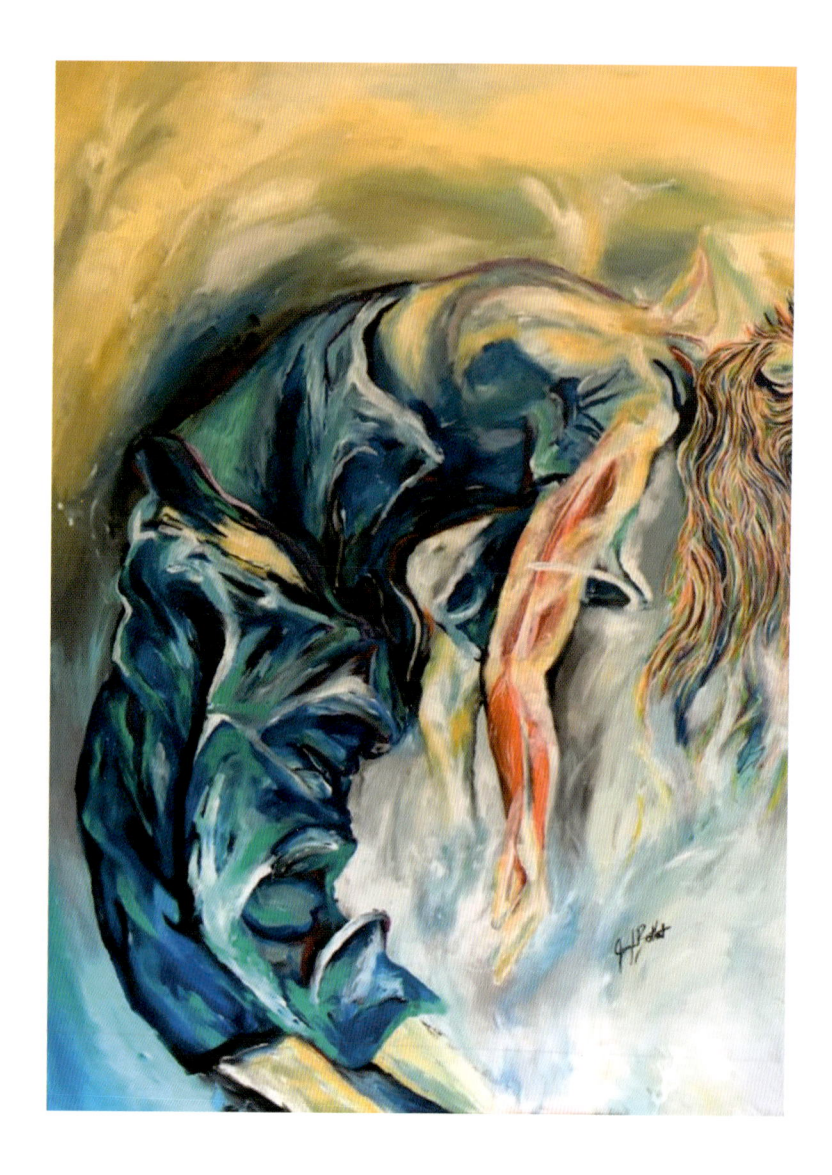

SURRENDERING TO SPIRIT • Jennifer Bothast • *Acrylic*

Surrendering to spirit can be more difficult than it should be. We want to control all the outcomes. We want to exert our own will and manifest all our desires. But what if we just got curious and surrendered this egocentric power trip to spirit, to the universe? What would it feel like to let go and trust? Transitioning perspectives can be just as powerful as moving between realms. (Truthtellers Exhibition, Spring 2018)

ON DEATH AND HOLDING
Jennifer Bothast

Dad died Saturday
with his belly in his chest,
his last breath
sounding like pudding thickened
in a pot. I've never watched anyone die all the way
before. Never had the "privilege" of presence
when the pain just stops.
When the last of his essence
quit begging for ice chips spooned like hops
onto his leathery tongue.

When the gurgling had been only a murmur—
before the last of his air leaked
out and we were
left. Before his body turned
off the autopilot well
of hitching and spasming for air.
We had been made witness to this war,
this quiet catastrophe, this private hell.
And after, when our own breath cooled into ribbons of heavy sighs and sobs,
I had searched for an apparition,
a flash of light or an orb.
But Dad had already left the room,
smiling softly while closing the door—
kissing his children on the head.
As if after having just tucked us all into bed,
he tip-toed away into the silence.

— Spring Series 2019, How the Light Gets In

(a) river rising • anthology of women's voices

LEST WE FORGET • Traci Mims • *acrylic on canvas*

Lest We Forget *is a reminder that we still have a lot of work to do in race relations. It looks at three generations of the same type of oppression. The images of Emmett Till, Yusef Hawkins, and Trayvon Martin symbolize the many who have suffered as the result of racism. Let us not forget them and the work we still need to do. (SHINE exhibition, Spring 2019)*

THE LOTTERY
Pat Geiger

That Monday night in December was an eerie one in downtown Kent, Ohio. The streets were nearly void of the usual throngs of university students lurking outside the bars and restaurants. Something more than darkness loomed over our heads.

Once past downtown, Steve grabbed my hand as we hurried across the railroad tracks and up the hill toward the fraternity house. Steve—tall, dark, handsome Steve. We had been dating for just under a year. I was attracted to his easy-going, fun-loving personality. He loved to party a bit too much. In fact, he was on the verge of flunking out of school.

Kegs were flowing, music was blaring—the excitement was palpable. It was lottery night at the Phi Kappa Theta house.

Steve threw $5 into the pot, which was already up to $84 and growing. The lucky guy with the right birthday would win it all.

At 8 o'clock, we all gathered around the television set in the living room. Sitting cross-legged on the floor, I scooted between Steve's legs and leaned against his chest. For a moment, I was sure I could feel his heart beating through his flannel shirt. I grabbed his slightly sweaty hands and wrapped his arms around me.

Anticipation was mounting as the numbers were about to be called. The crowd quieted down and a stillness enveloped the room. The first of the 366 blue plastic capsules (one for each day of the year, including February 29th) was about to be drawn by hand from the large glass container.

Sighs of relief and shouts of joy were audible with each number called. After a while, though, I noticed Steve starting to fidget. He scooted his legs out from around me and stood up. My stomach lurched as I saw his face turn pale. All eyes were on him as he smiled bravely and announced his "win," for his birthdate of October 5 was the first one called in our group.

The once jovial crowd turned sullen as reality set in. Heads lowered and eyes welled with tears. This would prove life changing for all of us. Much to his dismay, Steve had won the lottery. He would be the first of his fraternity brothers called up for the draft. You see, it was 1969 and this was the draft lottery, the first of its kind since World War II. Students in good academic standing were exempt from the draft. Those like Steve were eligible.

Steve did flunk out of college that winter. I recall a few late-night phone calls. He had indeed been drafted and adamantly insisted I not wait for him. The last call came right before he was sent to Vietnam. I saw right through his futile attempt at frivolity. I wished him well, told him I loved him, and made him promise to be safe. That was the last time I spoke to him. I'm sure I would have heard if he hadn't come back from the war. From time to time I think about Steve and pray that he was one of the lucky ones; that he didn't come back scarred, wounded, or destroyed. War is hell, and Steve was the first of my friends to discover that firsthand.

> *Kegs were flowing, music was blaring—the excitement was palpable. It was lottery night at the Phi Kappa Theta house.*

(a) river rising • anthology of women's voices

AFTERLIFE • Mary Atwood • *photography*

In 2018, my best friend of more than 40 years was killed in a tragic accident. **Afterlife** *was created as an expression of acceptance and a reflection on the transcendence of love over death. Through the use of macro photography, I was able to capture both the beauty and complexity contained in the withered white lily petals. The contrast between the dimly lit leaves and brightly lit petals is suggestive of the paradox of proximity and distance one experiences when mourning the death of a loved one.*

The contours of the upper petal were positioned to "embrace" the lower petal as a representation of the unbreakable bond of love. The spiraling end of the upper petal is an allusion to the continuum of creation. I chose to allow the lower petal to exceed the boundaries of the image to symbolize the unseen mysteries of the hereafter. The barely visible and faded green leaves in the background are an acknowledgement of the end of the physical life.
(RISE exhibition, Fall 2018)

VANISHING
Sharon Scholl

It's easier than I thought
now that I'm doing it

here among half-cleaned breakfast
dishes, my house taking on the day.

Laundry waits to be folded
sleeves dribbling from the plastic bin.

Your socks still turn up in the wash
tangled in sheets and towels

warm and shrunken from the dryer.
They are mine now, hug my feet,

having forgotten your size and shape.
Your wicker chest contains my clothes.

Everything is being translated
from duple into singular,

blended away like a lone cup
in a new stack.

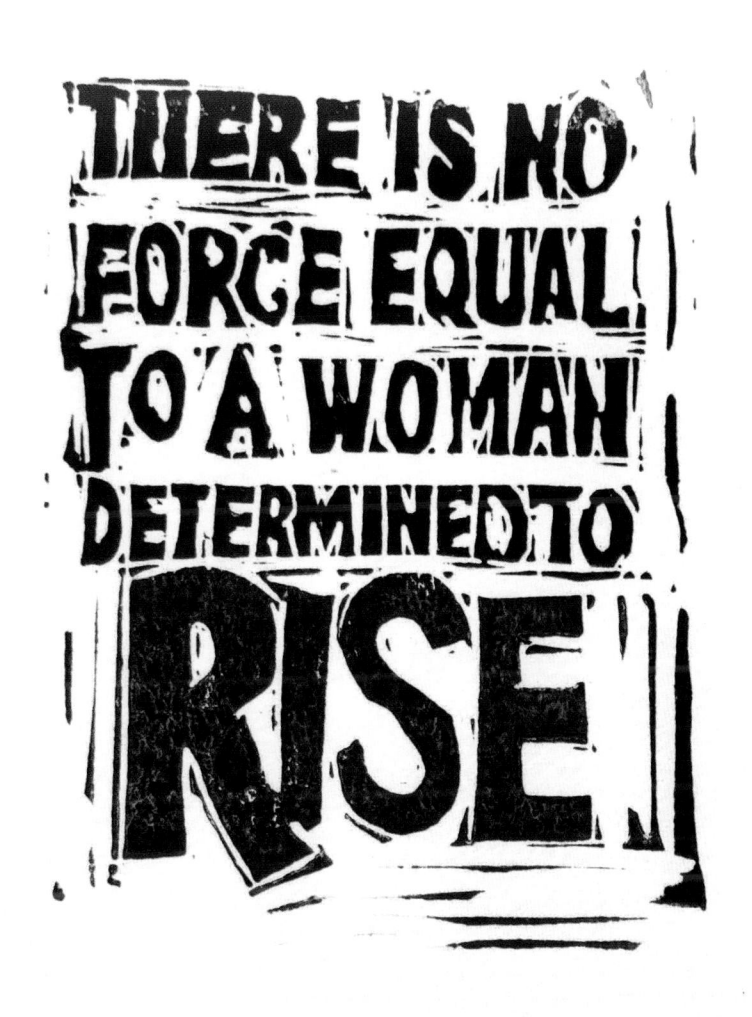

(a) river rising • anthology of women's voices

RISE • Hope McMath • *linocut*

This quote by the brilliant writer and civil rights leader W.E.B. Du Bois has inspired me for years as I've navigated a world that often works hard to keep me and other women in restrictive lanes. Our ability to lead, evolve, and build community requires determination, tenacity, compassion, and courage. The need and aspiration to rise up has power for us as individuals, but matters even more when it is a collective action. As impactful as these words are, how do they change when we alter "woman" to "women?" (RISE exhibition, Fall 2018)

STUDY FOR LADY IN GREEN • Erin Kendrick • *acrylic ink and Sharpie on canvas*

In my artwork, I challenge the historical perceptions of and about black women through the lens of the "oppositional gaze." The oppositional gaze is an intentional act of looking back, meant to challenge perceptions by becoming the spectator, as opposed to the spectacle, thereby reclaiming agency.

I feel I need to reclaim my identity from negative historical stereotypes and perceptions. I am trying to find ways in my artwork to portray black women's humanness vs. simply their blackness. I feel compelled, like so many other black women, to say: No—historically, people who look like me weren't just subservient, hyper-sexual, emasculating deviants. We were enslaved, sexually assaulted, long-suffering victims of trauma. While many things have changed, we are still bound by these perceptions through constant subtle signifiers in contemporary culture.
This is what attracted me to the notion of the oppositional gaze.

I paint using a process where I drop one to two colors of ink at a time, allowing it to stain the surface. I build up the paint, layer by layer, stain on top of stain. The staining represents the ideas, assumptions, perceptions, etc., that have defined black women's identity throughout history. My goal is to use those stains to reveal something beautiful, whole, and complete.

CONFLUX

Fourth Friday Series • Yellow House

TRUTH IS
(a found poem)

Truth is, I'm still getting used to
tying and untying the knots. I'm
tired of dealing with some people.
Life is hard.

Truth is, nothing really does get
solved. We have new things to
learn, and I have a right to tell my story.
I'm exhausted, but I'm at the beginning.

Truth is, I don't know what I'm doing
but I'll figure it out. Regardless, life
goes on. Sometimes you have to
revisit your past to get over it.

Truth is, I'm kinda scared…all the
time. I still go in that circle. I almost
didn't come tonight, but I'm really
glad I did.

Time doesn't heal all wounds
but my bitterest moments made
my sweetest moments that much
sweeter.

Truth is my very presence is truth.
This is what I tell myself.
I feel like I've lost so much, but we're
all part of the same tapestry.

I don't know. I'm still figuring it out.
That's been my whole life. Truth is,
I'm empowered by seeing other women's
power. I'm gonna get back

what is rightfully mine. Truth is the
truth, though some people would say
otherwise. Truth is hard sometimes.
Truth is.

You really can't change that.

—*Found poem by Jennifer Wolfe, from participants' words collected at a writing circle on women and race. (HER OWN THINGS exhibition, Yellow House, Summer 2018)*

(a) river rising • anthology of women's voices

NO LONGER SILENT • Jamie Galley • *mixed media*

As women unstitch our own lips, we can use our voices to turn anger and hurt into kindness and love directed toward collective healing. Can this chorus of truth and relentless love rip away the gossip, racism, sexism, homophobia, violence, and hate threaded into our culture? I think so. But it will take time and painful unravelling. Fabric frays and tears, but it can be mended and restitched to an even more beautiful whole.
(Yellow House Suffrage exhibition, Fall 2018)

Post-Election Writing Circle • Yellow House

BITTER
Hope McMath

Today I'm letting there be room for feeling bitter. Sharp, keep-me-awake-all-night, bad-taste-in-my-mouth bitter. And for this day, this moment, I am resisting my urge, and the urging of others, to wash it away with something sweet.

I am angry and disappointed again. I am stunned again. I am tired again. I am ready to resist, again. I need to give room for that bitter taste. Why not? This moment in time, and all the time before, seems marked, branded by hate. Hate wielded by a neighbor, the cashier at the store, the man sitting beside me in the waiting room, those I walk by on the street, those in power and those with none.

But I know that bitter is not my preferred food. I prefer joy, compassion, hard work, love, positive energy, and love. So I know I will not sit here for long. But I need to swirl this around in order to understand, to find motivation to continue the fight, and to know that this is not the place where I want to be. Until then, do not approach me with your "It's not so bad" because right now my "bitter" will burn it down.

—*Post-Election Circle: Yellow House, Nov. 7, 2018*

KEEP WALKING
Terri Neal

So much inner turbulence, again. I'm going to my first writing circle. What can my pen say to me, to others, on days like this? These were my first thoughts in my car on the way to the circle. Then I heard about Lucy McBath's congressional race in Georgia. She is taking the murder of her son, Jordan Davis, and using it to make wrongs right.

Then I remembered my grandmother. Grandmama would take shoes I'd outgrown and cut out the toes to make them fit. I could wear them a little longer until Mama could buy me more. My ancestors are used to this: using what we have to make what we need, until we have what we deserve.

Today, these shoes are ill-fitting. The shoes of injustice are too tight, painful. And yet, I will keep walking—even if I must cut the toes out of these shoes.

I .
I will.
I will make.
I will make something.
I will make something from.
I will make something from this.

—*Post-Election Circle: Yellow House, Nov. 7, 2018*

DEAR AMERICA
Phyllis Bell-Davis

Dear America, what kind of times are these?

Troublesome times are here, filling men's hearts with fear. Freedoms we all hold dear now are at stake. If we don't wake up out of this fear, we can never have a land that is free: free from oppression, homelessness, and other ills of society. These are troublesome times, not only because of party affiliation, but because of people's thoughts and mentalities.

When will we realize the reality of mortality and stop siding with political agendas? It's way past time. How can a country boast, "In God We Trust" and "God Bless America," placing hands over hearts—what's that all done for? Show?

Scripture says, "The greatest of all these is love." We say, "Love trumps hate." The problem is, we are without love. We kill each other because of gender and preferences. We kill our babies because they're defenseless. Where is the love for one another? I'm perplexed. It's a simple choice.

Dear America, what kind of times are these?

—*Post-Election Circle: Yellow House, Nov. 7, 2018*

(a) river rising • anthology of women's voices

ALTERNATIVE FACTS • Jennifer Bothast • *acrylic*

Who we think we are, what defines us, and the "reality" we see outside of ourselves is often just a set of lies we learned from our critics—especially that powerful critic we see in our own mirror. Conjuring a new word for a lie, such as calling it an "alternative fact," doesn't make it any less of a lie, no matter the source, and even it becomes a new, accepted political narrative. (Truthtellers exhibition, Spring 2018)

LESSONS FROM HISTORY
Beth Moore

Standing at the podium
Looking upon a sea of white faces in red hats
All chanting "Send her back!"
Smiling, 13 seconds he waited,
Resuming his speech, the noise abated.

Germany, 1932
Standing at the podium,
A small man with a pronounced mustache
Looking upon a sea of white adoring faces
"He is our savior, come to save us from poverty and early death."

The German experiment
To purify their race
Ended in the deaths of millions
All at a frightening pace.

The Jewish people
Slandered and slaughtered
Concentration camps became their home
Separation of families became the norm.

Some Germans took action to save the Jews.
Others looked on in horror but acted not
Still others joined in the rousing rallies
Emboldened to rid their country of people unlike them.

Here we are in 2019.
Different country, different time
The USA splitting apart
Egged on by its leader to
Hate those with colored skin, the Muslims, the Jews, and the queers too.
Withhold health care from those who are poor
And dark skinned refugees, bar the door.

"Do unto others as you would have them do unto you."*
"In as much as you did it not to one of the least of these, you did it not to me"**

These are the words of Jesus.
Where have all our Christians gone?

*Luke 6:31
**Matthew 25:45

I SAID "NO"
Amy Copeland

It's tough, the stuff
we go through, ya know?
Nah, I'm not talkin'
about the pain of childbirth
that's lame, compared to the
insane way
we have to live,
afraid to give for
fear of being taken!

When I was four,
I knew for sure I
wanted to be a boy
so I could pee standin' up—and
I was right 'cuz
now at night I
can't go out
without feelin' uptight.

At noon he drove up
askin' "Where's the
restroom?" It was just
him, me, and some
cars in that lot.
I fought him off,
alone. Back at home,
you said, "Get some rest,
but don't go there
or anywhere
without me."
I didn't agree.

"Did you think I
should be flattered—Each
time you approached
me? Even when
you held me down,
bit my breast, encroached
me? You shattered me
inside, for I
didn't have the strength or
heart left to fight when
you forced my legs apart
but I said, 'NO!'"

That's OK, I survived,
But inside, it kills me,
it ills me, makes me
wanna' beat the darkness
back. "No. You won't
torment my soul
today, the way
you misspent my youth.
No recompense
enough to soothe
the hurt you did to me."
I didn't agree.

—Surviving to Thriving event,
Women's Center of Jacksonville, April 2019

You shattered me inside, for I didn't have the strength or heart left to fight

Soul Circles • Jacksonville • Austin

WAKE UP
Linda Panetta

What does it mean to be awake? Really awake? Is it the responsibility of consciously awake women to find ways of encouraging others, to look deep within and stir up the questions that they might not want to think about—let alone answer? For me, I say yes. We are all connected in ways both large and small. As I continue to mature, I feel it necessary to perhaps ask the questions, not that I need to know the answers, so that maybe some of us—those that are ready—might think about this in many different ways and want to explore. So, as I continue to age, I will do what I can to help others live more consciously, more fully awake, and alive.

—*Art and Soul Series, Spring 2015*

ALIVE
Karen Knight

How alive am I willing to be?
I'm scared.

I'm seeking fullness
presence
feeling
depth.

Do I avoid/muffle/diminish
my fully alive-ness?

I think I want to be
fully alive…
Why do
I fear it?

How would it FEEL?
Awake. Vibrant. Visceral.

Is it that I can't handle being
FULLY ALIVE? There's
nowhere to
get to.

Is it eliminating distractions?
Eliminating
"deadening"
behaviors?

Wine. Laziness. Sluggishness
in bed. Lack of focus.

Lack of dedication. How do I
FOCUS fully on
CLARITY and
DESIRE

and utter ALIVENESS? What is that
feeling? Can I remain there

all the time? NOT sluggish
or FOGGY? What is
FULLY
alive?

Is it awareness? Acceptance?
Am I "there" yet? How to know?

Oh, the constant exhausting
STRIVING TO GET
THERE. Aren't we
"there" yet?
But YES! I wish to be MORE fully
alive, always more…exhausting

already! When is it ENOUGH?
Fully alive to me is
heightened
presence…

grace, ease, comfort, peace, joy…
in what IS.

EMBRACE it.
ACCEPT it.
LOVE it.
EXPERIENCE this moment NOW.

Always. That is being fully alive.
Grateful for this divine moment right now.

—*Song of the Soul Circle, Austin, Texas, Summer 2015*

What Love looks Like • Summer Van Mun

TRUTH
Karen Allen

The sun has not yet risen.
The blackness pervades.
Truth perches in the corner, naked.
She pierces my heart with her honest, emerald eyes
pleading with me to invite her to my warm bed.
The air moves as the fan twirls, yet neither her
golden hair, twisted lovingly with lavender irises,
nor the yellow daffodils on her crown move.

She is planted, firmly, in the corner.
Her arm reaches out and she writes in the air.
It's backwards though, like the word
AMBULANCE on the front of
emergency vehicles. I stare at her.
My heart lurches.
I'm wondering why it's backwards.

She full belly laughs at my unwillingness to meet
her gaze, and her head dances, splashing
lavender and golden swirls of light onto all
my bedroom walls. Do you want to know this
now, she queries, or later, when the only way
to read it will be in your rear view mirror?

Truth viewed in my rear view mirror is black
and white. Nothing like the golden goddess
planted here in the corner of my room.
The Truth in my rear view mirror hurts,
I finally say out loud. The pain pierces
my heart and my eyes leak tears.
Regret and shame run down
my cheeks and chin and drip onto
my chest, where they meet
forgiveness, sitting calmly in the garden
inside my heart. My breath catches
with vulnerability.

I tried so hard to make it work.
I gave everything, and I failed.
I bow my head unable to look at her.
She is Truth. She knows how much I tried.
All the hours and those copays,

Learning to manage his personality disorder,
placing my need for household calmness
above all else until my debt crushed me,
holding me hostage. The view is harsh
from my rear view mirror.
The lessons raw.

Truth in all her golden glory still perches
in the corner of my room.
She's quietly watching me, patiently waiting
for my decision. I notice my corner garden
has grown while I was peering into the
rear view mirror. Forgiveness is planted there
now, along with Compassion. As I take them in,
I'm astonished by their similarities.
They're actually twins and they sit arm-in-arm.
Pictures of me, I begin to notice, cover their
dresses. There I am in fifth grade writing
about love. I'm about three in that picture,
reading to my baby sister. And there's
the one of me covered in acne,
on Compassion's dress. Forgiveness has a photo
of the house key I returned to him
and she's written Courageous across the bottom.

I lift my head and look dead into Truth's emerald eyes.
I'm ready, I tell her, humbled by my rear view reverie.
Truth's emerald eyes twinkle as she
leans forward, ready to reveal what she's written
in the air. Each tender hand reaches up above her
head and grabs either end of the sentence she's
written. She crosses her outstretched arms in front
of her, turning my backwards truth around
so I can read it.

As I read her words, soft light slips slowly
through my blinds. I see her satisfied smile
through the letters as I read what she wrote.

"It's OK to trust yourself again" is now written
in the air of my room. I sigh and smile as she writes,
"Speak your Truth" across my open heart.

Truth • Karen Allen

WHAT LOVE LOOKS LIKE
Summer Van Mun

Do not think of me as selfish, please,
but I must share.
Your loving touch on my face,
your caress on my hair,
is not enough, my Dear.

It's been on my mind awhile now.
All this surface love will not suffice.
It will not quench my desire
to dive deeper with you
past the blue sea
into the darkness of me.

I want to feel your warm embrace
around E-V-E-R-Y cell of my being.
I want you to cherish everything—
including the imperfect things
that do not come out right.
The very things I myself try to fight.
I want to feel your acceptance
after you drink in my soul,
and lick the bitterness off your lips—
saying it adds to the glow
of my radiance.

I want you to see my fear, Love—
and love my fear.
I want you to understand
and swaddle my fear.
Tell me it will be okay, Dear.

I want you to see my rage, Love—
and love my rage—
understand and marvel at my rage.
Know and not fear how powerful I am.

I want to let my tears free fall in front of you
without awkwardness or apology.
I want you to love the grief I show.
And I want to know that there is no depth of
my soul that you are not willing to go.
I want you to allow me to surround you
in this dance of darkness—
putting out the fire of my desire,
feeling the safety of knowing me fully,
becoming the ether that rises off
the hot coals of our burning love affair.

And then, then
I want you to kiss my pretty face,
stroke my hair—
loving me completely in this place.

—*Maintain Your Writer's Shape drop-in circle, Fall 2014*

ODE TO JIM
Lisa Weatherby

Damn, what is with me?
Can't get over you.
The ups and downs
are making me blue.

Confusion and drama
leave us both so conflicted.
A constant reminder
of the pain you've inflicted.

You love me and leave me
and I won't hear a word
for weeks, maybe months.
It's just so absurd.

You belong with your family
so leave me alone.
You can't have it both ways.
Lord, I should have known.

DEFINITIONS
Tracy Ann Miller

An actress almost before I could walk, learning lines before kindergarten. Curtain! Lights! You see what I want you to see. I want you to see what pleases you.

Schoolgirl days and I am an amalgamation of course subjects, teams, and clubs. Fast-moving, always growing. See me hiding behind my books and understand me through them.

Know me by the roles I play: daughter, sister, friend. The smart one, never the pretty one, never the star. I grow my hair long like a shield. Pretend your rejection doesn't hurt. Move on to the next audition.

I try on characters. Play bigger venues. Indulge my own tastes as the ingénue. You see what I want you to see. I want you intrigued. Awards on my mantle. A degree. A marriage. Label me overachiever.

What happened to all the good scripts? Wait. Pull the curtain. Sacrifice. Lose my favorite titles: Charlestonian, followed by wife. Look in the secret, quiet places and discover the ache, the title I have been denied. Mother.

Know me then by my losses, by the paralyzed places in my heart. Death. Separation. Call me the Ice Queen; you will not be the first. Fear the darkness in me. Beware the cold depths of the inky ocean of sorrow. The stage is empty.
Nothing to see here.

Embrace the stillness. Understand me by my faith and call me Witch. Seek me out backstage with my curious experiments. Study the formulas and chemistry.
I am the teacher, the healer.

Patience. Look under the fencer's mask. Know me by my blade. I am the Warrior. Knight of Honor. Me for you. Your name forever safe in my presence. Steadfast.

Curtain up. What do you see? Recall the flames I lit for you and how together we built them into vast bonfires. Know me by the love I gave.

Define me now by what love made possible.

Stories From Home • Riverside Avondale Preservation Society

LEMON MERINGUE PIE
Melody Jackson

It was a time when I was a child—no, middle-school age. Every day, I came home to a home-cooked meal. My mom, humming in the kitchen, would yell out, "Go wash your hands and come back to the table!"

This was every single day of my adolescent life. There was always perfectly steamed white rice; luscious vegetables, like squash or cabbage, always mixed with onions and bell peppers. She'd bring my plate to me, the meat falling off the sides, covered in gravy.

But the best was yet to come! Oh, her homemade lemon meringue pie, with its perfectly browned foam egg white tips! (Beaten by hand, I later learned.) This was it! I'd hurry through my meal just to get to dessert.

That gorgeous yellow lemon filling and that sparkling white meringue with its brown tips—yes, it was baked most perfectly. She never seemed to tire of making it, ever.

Then one day, I heard her tell my auntie, "I never have liked cooking!"

She taught me well. By doing what she hated so well, she always reminds me to keep doing my best.

—Stories From Home circle, Fall 2017

WHERE I'M FROM
Shinnerrie Jackson

I am from washing machines,
from Windex and Comet.
I am from the quiet country suburbs
(serene, kind, with
pine needles and moving cars).
I am from moonlit jasmine,
pungent and clean.

I'm from sit-down meals and hard work
      from Frances and Yearty Pringle
I'm from the violence
      and the affection,
from steadfast faith and cleanliness.
I'm from Jesus is the way
      and make your own way.

I'm from Cowford and Starke,
fried chicken and snap peas,
from the rough sharecropping
      train-building hands
the washboard-run-down fingers.

I am from those moments—
stored in attics, albums, and
ottomans
never to be brought out or explained.

—Inspired by the poem, "Where I'm From," by George Ella Lyon

PROMPT
What reminds you of home?

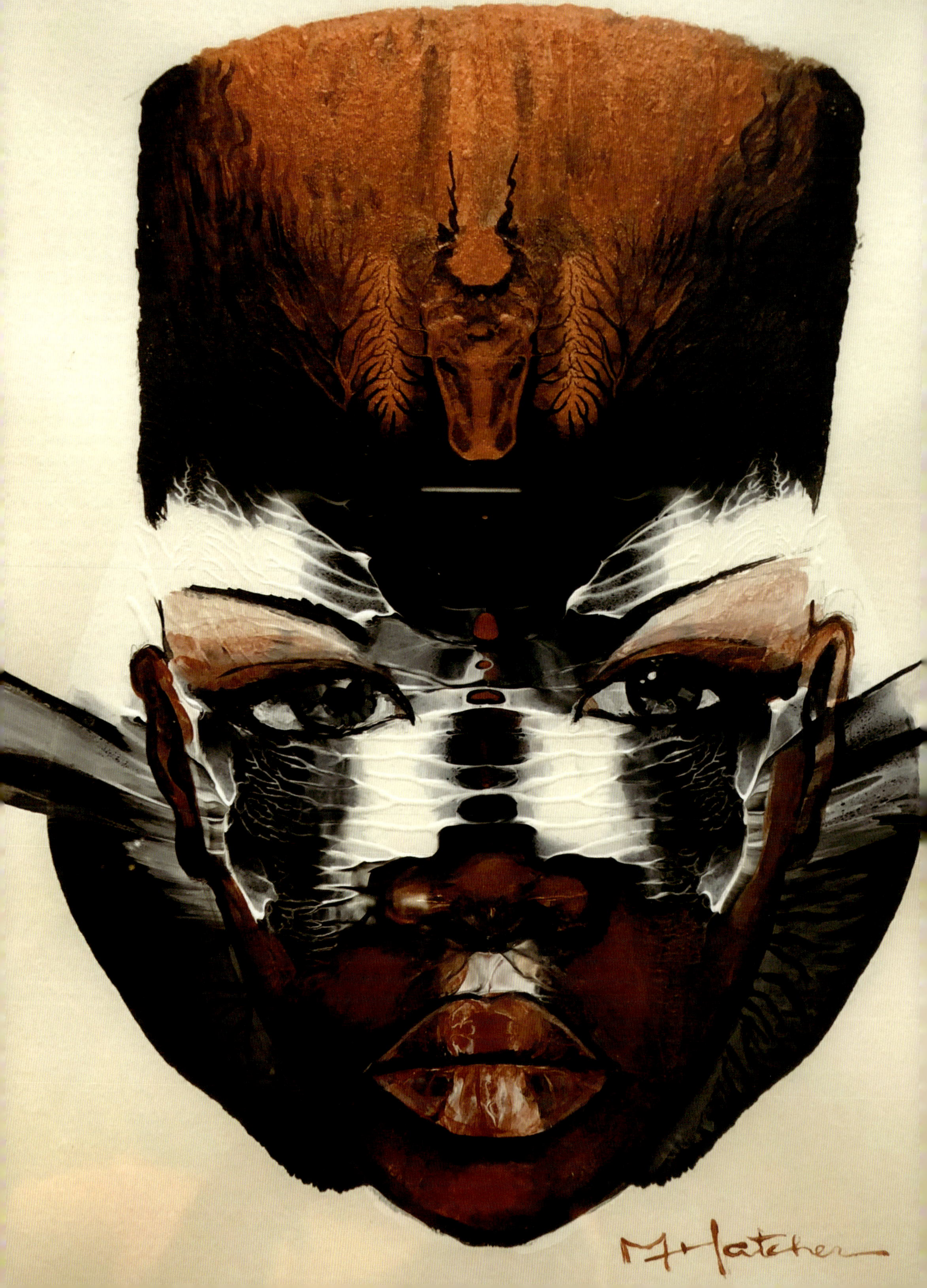
M Hatcher

APARTHEID
Cathy Courtney

Nelson Mandela was locked up in Robin Island prison when I was in South Africa—just a name among many others who were persecuted or murdered for interfering with the Apartheid government.

I was sheltered as a child, tucked away in a British Anglican girls' boarding school. It is only when I grew up that I began to make sense of what happened in my childhood.

The pot was boiling in the 1960s. Rioting was everywhere and South Africa was a dangerous place to be. Sanctions from around the world—a rude awakening, shaming me into realizing that I was one of those bad guys. We had black "servants" at home and I loved them. I remember Alf, our gardener, proudly showing off his biceps at my requests when friends came over! Three of his wives came to work for us at different times. As one got pregnant and left, the next would arrive to take her place. Tina, my favorite, would sit on my bed in the mornings, listening with eager fascination to what I told her about what I had learned in school. She had no education.

My father was British-born, which made us British subjects. My two older sisters emigrated, while I stayed behind to support my mother as my father's cancer advanced. Quite soon after he died, in the mid 70s, my mother and I went to join my sisters in London.

My best friend and college roommate had a brother (white, of course) who became a doctor in South Africa. He went to work at an overcrowded all-black hospital and started advocating for the rights of the black people. He was imprisoned and hung himself in jail. It was said to be a suicide but was later identified as torture. Traumatized, my friend and her family left for England.

I'd always felt I was British in South Africa. We followed all the British traditions at home and I went to a British school. Sunday roast dinners were delicious and, of course, there was hot tea and scones. But I was not well received by the British people for some time because of the country I was connected to.

Apartheid eventually caved in. Nelson Mandela was freed from prison and became the new Prime Minister of South Africa—a shining example of forgiveness for the cruel sentence he had endured.

After 14 years of living in London, I moved to America. Although it has become my new home, a part of me still feels British at heart. My family is still in England, and perhaps because of that, I will always have that connection.

I have not been back to South Africa. I'm sad to see it is still troubled by corruption. Such a beautiful country, with such enormously complex problems.

—Memoir Series, Fall 2017

. . . . .

GRACE AND THE BULL • Marsha Hatcher • *acrylic*

We go through life looking but not seeing, listening but not hearing. What I see and what you see can and often are totally different. Things are not always what they seem. I call the images in this series **Canucwhatic** *— Can You See What I See? The work is based on Rorschach's ink blot test, but instead of ink, I use paint and color to add dimension. This is not a psychological test but more of a vision test for art lovers. I often use this method of painting with children as a way to encourage creativity. Free-flowing paint is strategically added to paper, which is then folded in half with slight pressure to distribute the paint. The paper is slowly opened to reveal the image. Most images are obvious but some are not. By adding facial features to the image, I am able to show the viewer exactly what I see. (RISE exhibition, Fall 2018)*

Community Voices • Outreach

THE LIE-BERRY
Jennifer Thornton

The lie-berry—what a perfect name for a place you can go and lie to yourself. Lie to yourself about who you are for hours on end, nourishing yourself with berries of knowledge.

The lie-berry is a complex labyrinth of information. In each text is a portal to another dimension, where you can lose your identity. There you become someone you've always fantasized about being, or even someone who the very thought of being terrifies you.

Before each new adventure, I find it necessary to tether myself to something tangible in this version of reality, just in case I get lost so I can climb back into this universe, where my mundane responsibilities are too routine. I can dive into a new character and become so immersed in its features I forget to eat for days. I feast on the words I'm putting into my mind, and my intellectual metabolism converts the words into fuel.

'Cause the lie-berry. It's only a lie if you don't believe it.

—*Fourth Fridays at the Jax MakersSpace in the Jacksonville Public Library downtown*

PEBBLES ON A BEACH
Manisha Joshi

Pebbles on the beach
scattered on the sand,
like memories washed away
and brought back onto the land.
Hear the sound of the crashing tides
when the moonlight hits, the sunshine hides.
Endless waves come
and crawl back in again,
like moments that once started,
like moments that have to end.
Pearls hidden in oysters
are often out of reach,
like voices silenced by time
that cannot recognize speech.
The scenery of moods
changes as the waves do.
They come like a cherished jewel
and are tossed like an old shoe,
Ah, the smell of salty waters
the thought of swimming them,
like an impulsive desire
that leads to a suppressed end.
Oh, I cherish the moments of today,
I fear not to say why.
I find joy in living today
for tomorrow I may die…

—*Soul on Fire Retreat, January 2019*

INNER CHILD
Lena Crowe

When I was 10 years old, my mom went away on a work trip. She returned with a dangly, grey, fuzzy, stuffed-animal hippo who was soon dubbed "Hippie." At the time, my favorite animals in the entire world were hippos (they still are!). I was so passionate about them at that age, that I even curated a website for kids that was solely about hippos. I worked so tirelessly on that website! My parents assisted me with scanning the comic strips I drew, I wrote a fictional story about Ken the Purple Hippo and all of his friends, and I gathered facts related to hippos. Hippie essentially became the mascot of the website. Now Hippie represents everything about my childhood, especially my creativity and passion for writing. Hippie went everywhere with us—we have pictures of her at our cabin in North Carolina, in Honduras, etc. Hippie always stood out to me the most out of all my stuffed animals; I gave them all away except for her. I still have her and know exactly where she is in my apartment, sitting on a chair waiting for the next time I need to hold her when I'm upset. Hippie represents a lot to me—my childhood, my relationship with my mom, my writing, and my comfort. While Hippie represents my childhood, and I guess I'm an adult now, that doesn't mean she represents the finalization of my childhood—it means that she is a piece of that inner child in me that will never fully go away. She'll always be a friend there to comfort me. Whether I'm 10 or 100, I will always wrap her in my arms whenever I cry.

—*Writing Through Transitions Circle, Spring 2019*

Care of the Container • Caring for the Community

LETTER TO A WRITER

Janessa Martin

To Whomever Needs This:

Take this class. Take it. Forget the rumblings of the mind—I can't write, I have nothing to say, I'm unworthy.

Click the button—YES.

Drive past the writer's house if need be the week before. Wring your hands. Wreak havoc with the little red devil playing on your shoulder. Peruse your calendar and count too many commitments. The excuses, yes, they will come.

But, please oh please, show up.

Let the love in this room envelope you. The authenticity of these women, circled round, pen in hand, uplift you. The you you may have forgotten or thought was venturing forth alone. The one who you promised to honor as a little girl. Yes, bring her. Bring a pen and let the words flow onto paper.

Take this class. Take it. Forget the rumblings of the mind—I can't write, I have nothing to say, I'm unworthy.

Click the button—YES.

Editor's Note: Women Writing for (a) Change uses the practice of an occasional "care of the container" circle to help participants comment, in writing, about the work they're doing in the circle and how the process is working for them. This is a small selection of those writings.

WRITING TO CHANGE THE WORLD — Jackie Casey

This writing class has affected my view not only of the world that surrounds me, but also the world that surrounds other women. Like-minded or not, I have learned that other women are learning to speak up. I am as well. I have learned that we are more alike than we think. I have learned that writing brings pure joy to my soul. I have learned that when women get together, there is lots of laughter and that the laughter brings out the light, casts out the darkness. I have learned that the light is encapsulating and penetrating, a real soul-shaker and movement-maker.

Writing brings us together. We truly connect by listening to our peers, combining our poetry through Readback lines, and critiquing each other's work—in a judgment-free atmosphere. The world that lies in front of my writing-self is a world with many possibilities. Where pen meets paper, it is love at first sight.

CARE OF THE CONTAINER — Linda Mahoney

How have the roles rituals and processes of the circle helped me with my writing?

I'm reminded of the giant trees in California whose roots are webbed together such that one tree can give nourishment to another. Our thoughts are connected as we sit in the circle and write. We each have voice and a point of view, but there is a shared reality because of the roles and rituals. The calm and care is visibly present.

Acceptance and support are the norm. Humor is the welcome friend we hope shows up. A laugh and a twinkle in the eye are just the relief we all need. We are free from the monstrous stress of the day. Have we done enough?

In the circle, the writing is timed. It IS enough. No need for perfection or achievement. There is joy in the process. There is joy in knowing the rituals will keep us safe and provide that natural harmony so we can bring our voices together. We are different, and diversity brings creativity. We are also alike as we are participate in the human experience. experience.

GLORIA WHO? • Joyce Gabiou • *mixed media*

This piece is dedicated to the women's movement, led by Gloria Steinem and others. It calls attention to the fact that Gloria is little known by younger feminists despite the fact that they have reaped the rewards of the work done by Gloria and her fellow female leaders.
(The Art of Memoir exhibition, Fall 2017)

FAST GIRL
Lanette Frank

I forgot how much I love to drive fast.
Fast cars with muscle, guts, speed,
design, flow. A sports car where the seat fits
the body snugly and the steering wheel fits
my arms at just the right length,
with a slight bend in the elbow, for
quick maneuvering. It feels good when the
right touch at the right time on the gear
shifter causes it to slide into place at the exact
right moment. I push my foot down on
the accelerator, hard, and the car leaps forward
in response to my command, like
a lover under my spell,
who does what I ask of him,

weaving in and out of traffic
or wide open on the interstate.
Pushing the needle higher
always testing, testing how fast
I'm willing to go. "Aren't you going a bit fast?
Shouldn't you slow down?"
"Shut the hell up," is my only response.
No external critic permitted. No
internal critic allowed, looking for safety.
I turn the loud thumping music up louder,
good fucking times
just me alone.
A fast girl
in a fast car...

If there were no ring on my finger and
vow on my lips
I would fuck who I wanted
when I wanted.
He'd be younger, if only by a day
And funny, smart, and interesting, of course
I'd always pay for dinner.
He'd never stay the night.
Alas, I don't lie, cheat, or steal,
I drive a beater, covered in sand
from the beach and hair from my dogs
and I love one man madly.
No apologizing allowed,
this is who I am.

I was born this way,
a fast girl who likes fast cars.

—*Summer Adventure, Little Talbot Island State Park, Summer 2019*

AMATERASU • Elena Ohlander • *acrylic and archival ink on birchwood*

Amaterasu is the Goddess of the Sun and the sister of Tsukuyomi, the Goddess of the Moon , and Susano'o, the goddess of the Sea and Storms. She is in charge of Takamagahara, or the High Celestial Plain, the dwelling of all gods. Without her light to shine upon the world, it would plunge into darkness. (SHINE exhibition, Spring 2019)

SHINE

How the Light Comes

Shana Brodnax

How the light comes, for me, is by being willing to be in the dark as long as it takes. Some things you only learn in the dark.

I finally learned—when I tumbled all the way down to the bottom of a well, after turning away from its darkness over and over for years and years—that the things in the dark don't go away just because you ignore them. I didn't get out of that well until I emptied it, even though I had to do it with a teacup. I didn't get out until I turned toward the darkness, until I saw what there was to see—what I hadn't been willing to see. I didn't get out until I stopped resisting and tensing and straining— and started breathing. Started allowing. Started softening. Started feeling.

I thought feeling everything down there in the darkness would kill me, but it didn't. It did open me—and when I finally emerged into the light, there were new places in me for the light to fill.

So I don't fear the darkness anymore, or avoid it, or demonize it. When I have to go down to the dark, I don't build a house there, but I surrender to the time and process that it requires, and the purpose that it serves.

Some things you can only learn in the dark.

—*How the Light Gets In, Spring Series 2019*

POPPIES • Bronwen Chandler • *acrylic on canvas*

Poppies in their vibrant glory reflect the brilliant effect of light and illuminate our inner being with their beauty. (SHINE exhibition, Spring 2019)

MATTHEW DUG A HOLE
Jennifer Wolfe

I wanted to bury Buster in the backyard, in the garden. My son, Matthew, agreed. When I came home that afternoon, he said he'd found the perfect spot. It was under the palm tree, just beyond the outer circle of the patio. I concurred; it was perfect.

Last summer, I was working with a handyman on a project to dig a trench around the house. I asked Matt to help him. At 21 years old, he was reluctant. He didn't want to get up early. He didn't want to deal with digging up the tangled roots. He didn't want to push through and do the job properly. I was chagrined.

So when I asked him to dig a hole for Buster's grave to prepare for a tiny funeral, I had my doubts. But I left him alone; I needed to prepare my program before my friend, Beth, and her daughter, Avery, arrived for the service. Avery got there first, carrying a plate of homemade cookies and a pot of yellow mums. I checked on Matt and saw he was still struggling, having to cut through the landscape cloth and the thick roots underneath it. I still needed to finish my own work, however, so again, I left him alone.

Finally, I was ready with my one-page program—a mix of some relevant quotes and a sweet poem written by a writing circle friend. My plan was to ask Avery to hold the flowers and Beth to hold the candle; I would hold the ukulele to accompany us for the singing parts, and Matt would hold Buster. But I worried; would the hole be deep enough? Had Matt properly completed the job?

Checking one last time, I walked to the edge of the garden, noting a large pile of dirt. I looked into the hole Matthew had dug, and saw that it was perfect. Deep, narrow, just the right size, in just the right spot. I was gratified. Asking still more of Matthew, I said, "Would you please go get Buster?" Buster had been lying "in state" in his well-worn doggy bed, upstairs, next to my own bed.

Matt brought him down to me, wrapped in a blue towel, with just Buster's ears sticking out. We proceeded to the backyard, with Matthew in front, gravedigger and pall bearer all at once.

We lit the candle, sang Amazing Grace, and read the poem. I cried unabashedly. Then I kissed Buster's ears one final time and Matthew laid him in his grave. We went inside and left Matthew to finish the job, the candle burning in the softly falling darkness.

...imprinting the world with his own loving touch, petting Buster one final time.

Later, I checked on Buster a final time. The candle was still lit and glowing in the dark, and the hole neatly filled in. I saw Matthew had also left a handprint in the soft dirt, imprinting the world with his own loving touch, petting Buster one final time.

I could ask no more of him. He had done what I asked him to do, and then, he did more. Matthew dug a hole, and he filled it in, his own particular way. Such is the everyday grace, the amazing grace, of being lost, then found.

Here. In the garden.

PORTRAIT OF MY MOTHER
Karen Erren

Today I went to the library. I go most Saturdays. I love the library—I love to read. I missed my mom so deeply today. She, too, was an avid reader.

I remember when I was a little girl, my mother would close herself in her room for hours, with the door shut tight. When I knocked, she would say "Just a minute!" and I would hear her purposeful rustling before that space opened to me. Or (I think, with the hazy uncertainty of some childhood memories) that sometimes she just didn't let me in, though I don't remember what words she used to send me away. I would listen mightily outside the door, but there were never any clues as to what was going on within.

When I snuck through the large white louvered doors into her closet one day to locate the source of this secrecy, I found brown grocery store bags filled with Harlequin romances. The thin ones with the cover of the breathless damsel held by the brawny, well-oiled leading man—bosoms and arms both bulging.

In many ways, my mother's story was the ultimate romance. Carol Mann, Southern girl from a small town; doesn't debut by choice, goes off to a two-year finishing school college in the Midwest and dates...foreign exchange students.

My great-grandparents pretty much raised my mother. Partner, as we called her grandfather, was a vocal opponent of school integration in

WEDDING PORTRAIT
provided by Karen Erren • *photography*

Carol Mann Gannaway Eruren and Guner Eruren, September 9, 1961

Portrait of My Mother • Karen Erren

Little Rock in the late 1950s. My mother was a member of "the lost class," which is what they called the high school students who couldn't graduate in 1959 because the schools were closed by order of the Arkansas governor. She spent her senior year in a small town about fifty miles from home. Until the day she died, she wouldn't talk about that year, so I still don't know what made it so bad. She wrote about it for a class once, when she was getting her master's degree, but she wouldn't let me read what she wrote.

After her senior year of high school and a summer at home, she left by train for Columbia, Missouri. The old saying is that a girl goes to Stephens College to get her "MRS." My mother did meet the love of her life there. He was at the University of Missouri, having wrangled permission to study in the United States at a time when his home country did not allow it.

Arriving in the United States, Daddy changed colleges on his trip from New York to St. Louis, instantly abandoning his plans for engineering school in Rolla when the guy sitting next to him on the plane told him it was a men-only school. He wound up at the University of Missouri, Columbia, and my beautiful redheaded mother, ten years his junior, caught his eye across the room at a party. And so Carol Mann brought home a fella, from Istanbul, with a pencil-thin mustache and oiled-back hair. We always say he looked like King Farouk, who ruled Egypt and the Sudan in the 1930s. I am certain that he was the first Turk ever in the state of Arkansas those many years ago, in the early 1960s.

I tell you all this to say—in my mind, Daddy was mother's biggest adventure. They enjoyed a lifetime of travel together. For the last twenty years of their marriage, they took multiple trips each year all around the globe. But after the stroke he had in Croatia in 2011, Daddy's 81-year-old self was content to be at home: Wake-breakfast-walk dog-garden-lunch-nap-coffee-errands-happy hour-dinner-sleep. The adventures were over.

Did my mom see a vast expanse of same stretching ahead, trapping her within that 1,700 square foot home? Did she see a relentless pace of hours, days, weeks, months, years, maybe decades?

We'll never know why she climbed up to the hall closet that night. What was she reaching for, perched on that little bitty slick-leather topped 1970s barstool? We will never know the reason, but climb she did. And she fell, and broke her neck, and died.

I tell you all this to say— in my mind, Daddy was mother's biggest adventure.

I had spoken to her less than two hours before—calling, as I usually did, on the way home from the office. I thank God THAT night I did not slip over into that specific impatient and contemptuous language that flows so easily between mother and daughter—the ready irritation that comes from knowing she is a part of your very cells—just outside your body, not within. Still heartbeat-connected, from so many years before. I thank God I told her I loved her.

My mom was vastly interested in other people. Her family, friends and neighbors attest to her thoughtfulness, generosity and insatiable love of experiencing life. My oldest daughter says, "She was a part of every adventure I ever had." Among many other things, she lived a great romance and traveled the world, both on her trips and through her beloved books.

I miss her. I think of her every single day.
And always in libraries.

DELIBERATE (AUDRE LORDE) • Sylvi Herrick • *oil on linen*

This painting is from a series on "brazen libertine women." Beautiful, strong, outspoken, they drove me to be courageous and live my life fearlessly. I decided to paint some of my antiheroines when I needed them the most, in 2016. This painting is not a portrait but inspired by images patched together from other reproductions available in the public realm. Female bodies as the repository of knowledge and power. I have painted them from the perspective of a lover, not a voyeur. Erotic, yes, pornographic, no. Naked, yes, nude, no. Composition, though underrated, is critical. Negative space is full of possibility. The palate is murky, muddy, earthy hues with a blast of cool springtime beauty. (Truthtellers exhibition, Spring 2017.)

JANUARY CHILD
Mary Warren

I came along in the dead of winter, blizzard raging,
born in my own time three weeks late.
Father was at work.
Mother begged a ride from the man next door
to go and do her woman's work alone.
She napped me on the porch
to be toughened by the snows
and gales of January, to cut my teeth
on New England nor'easters
and prepare for the undeclared war against girls.
Middle child, only girl, small for my age.

Both brothers slept the porch in spring
took for granted the abundance
of our neighborhood, the visitors and friends,
the elms and hyacinths, maples and forsythias,
new hues of green,
the migratory flocks parading back to northern homes.
Both boys read books, played quiet games,
grew fat on father's favor.

I grew to a storm-wintered warrior child
sight practiced on bare lilac thicket, schooled
by wind in how the world sounds, cries
accompanied by jays and blackbirds,
layered against the elements.
Perhaps my fights were attempts to win
that unwinnable war
but I fought with the fury of calling,
battered brothers' enemies
and marshaled anger from hidden fronts
as I gave birth to myself.

ANHELO
Sonja M. Álvarez

Anhelo…	I long…
Anidar mis pies descalzos	to nest my bare feet
En la emblemática falda	on the iconic skirt
De un flamboyán manso	of a meek flamboyán tree
Con alas desde el suelo	wings from the ground
Altísimas cual la barca	so high as the vessel
Que navega en mi regazo	that sails on my lap
Anhelo…	I long…
Un templo llamado campo	for a temple called Countryside
Allí donde las aves trinan	there where the birds warble
Las niñas se hacen mozas	where Girls become Dames
Los viejos se hacen santos	the Old become Saints
En una montaña lluviosa	on a rainy mountain
De mi Isla del Encanto	from my Island of Enchantment
Anhelo…	I long…
El embate de las olas	for the onslaught waves
Amurallándose en auroras	of wallowing auroras
Del insolente pájaro de acero	that insolent steel bird
Atándole al espíritu el lazo	ripping the ties
Donde el corazón desboca	amongst spirit and hearts
A la locura del ocaso	posing soul facing the seas
Anhelo…	I long…
Ese horizonte pintado	for the Meztizo blue tones
En tonos de azul mestizo	of a that painted horizon
Cual las penas del exilio	as the exiled sorrows
Que se arrojan a la fosa	jump into the trench
Del corazón que posa	of the heart that poses
Su alma frente al mar	a soul facing the sea
Anhelo…	I long…
La mirada alta	to look over
Sobre el pesado abismo	the heavy chasm
De quienes se van	of those who leave
Y los que se quedan,	and those who stay,
Aquel pebetero y altar	that intense cauldron and altar
Que es mi Viejo San Juan	that's My Old San Juan

SO MANY PLACES
Rachel Kohl

I have been to dogfights on the Redneck Riviera
cockfights in Puerto Rico

I have been to rattlesnake round ups
flounder gigging by spotlight

I have been to snow white sand beaches
submerged in salty blue water

I have been to the bottom of the Grand Canyon
hiked out by moonlight

I have been to Mount Desert Island in Acadia
rose early to catch first sunrise

I have been for weeks in trailer parks in Mexico
rented condos for months in California

I have been to hear BB King in Portland
I heard him again in Copenhagen

I have been to New Orleans for a Mardi Gras ball
missed it when the bus broke down in Slidell

I have been to the town of Middlefart on the way to the island of Funen
seen the word "slut" covered to protect the queen

I have been to Hawaii for R and R
Toronto for New Year's Eve

I have been to Wiesbaden as consultant for hire
Germans there seldom said hi

I have been to Harvard to work for a professor
at MIT I worked for a computer

I have been to Cambridge to teach a class
reverence made me whisper

I have been to so many places
now pleasingly I'm planted in Springfield

ONCE UPON A TIME
Woody Winfree

Once upon a time, I believed in a crazy kind of magic. Magic powerful enough to do unimaginable things, like stopping cancer in its tracks.

My faith in such sorcery arose spontaneously one harried day when I stopped to get gas. Harried, because I was heading to the hospital to take on the role, once again, as a kind of cancer first-responder for a loved one.

I took control of my own breast cancer, making decisions that were clear-cut and successful for me. But frustration characterized my inability to carve a healthy cancer-free path for others dear to me.

As I prepared to pump the gas that day, my distracted thoughts were interrupted by the squawking box inquiring, "Would you like a car wash with your fill-up?" With the punch of a button, I answered "Yes," something I rarely do.

That "yes" materialized out of a frazzled construct of helpless reasoning and hapless wishing: keeping my car clean is something I can control, and I could parlay that control directly into influencing the health of my family and friends. This made perfect sense at the time.

With my tank full and carwash code in hand, I pulled into the fun house of water jets and drums that spit and slap cars clean. The fun was short-lived. Continued distraction caused me to nick my front fender inching into the washing zone. How bad could it be? It was a question that could have been answered soon enough, but instead I opened my door for a quick look.

Bam! The four-foot drum of streaming plastic red tendrils jumped into service, meeting my open car door broadside. After several futile attempts to push it back while standing in my new cork-soled leather shoes in the rising water, I realized the only way out was forward.

Safely outside, having abandoned the spit and shine of the wash, I checked for damage. My relief at finding that my door opened and closed abrutly turned to despair as I sighted a shaft of sunlight coming through the doorjamb.

Suddenly, I got a new take on my reality. From the sound of the drum hitting my open door, the feel of my soaked shoes, and the blindness I had even now to the massive machinery moving behind me, I could hear, feel, and see how truly out-of-control I was. From this highly charged place of errors, helpless

> *That "yes" materialized out of a frazzled construct of helpless reasoning and hapless wishing: keeping my car clean is something I can control...*

frustration, and embarrassing carelessness, I gave way to complete resignation.

Once again, I knew that the only way out was to move forward.

After a restless night, I arrived first thing the following morning at Rocko's Auto-Clinic. I stepped out of my car, into this masculine garrison of heavy metal, sporting my second-skin yoga wear that, I often forget, doesn't render me actually clothed in the public arena.

"Wow, your body looks great!" said the hulking, bald-headed man emerging from the car next to mine. Perhaps it was my exhaustion from tossing through

Once Upon a Time • Woody Winfree

the night with visions of a $2,000 repair bill that tempered my response. Another time, like over the past 40 years of armored feminism, I would have snapped back with an indignant retort.

Instead, I received this observation about my 60-year-old body as the nicest thing I had thought or heard about myself over the previous 24 hours. Instead of a rant, I said, "Thank you. I need some help."

Help appeared in the form of Rocko himself. The owner of the body shop was none other than the man I chose not to tear into for his comments about my physical appearance.

After 30 minutes of jiggering an alignment tool and applying brute force, my cock-eyed door was straight as an arrow and my bruised ego lifted with it. The moment turned even sweeter when I asked him what I owed. "Just give me a tip," he replied.

Transformed from being hardened by life and being hard on myself, I turned playful: "Always brush your teeth before going to bed at night."

Rocko threw his bald head back with laughter. He said this advice was lost on him. His mouth was fitted with dentures: two rows of false teeth replacing his own enameled ones lost to years of homelessness, with no place to brush his teeth before bed.

In that moment, real magic occurred. It appeared not in the form of cancer cures created by clean cars, but in the form of human connection created by kindness, and a little humor. Standing in the shade of my dirty car, an unlikely pair, we hugged.

PROMPT
When have you experienced moments of grace with a stranger?

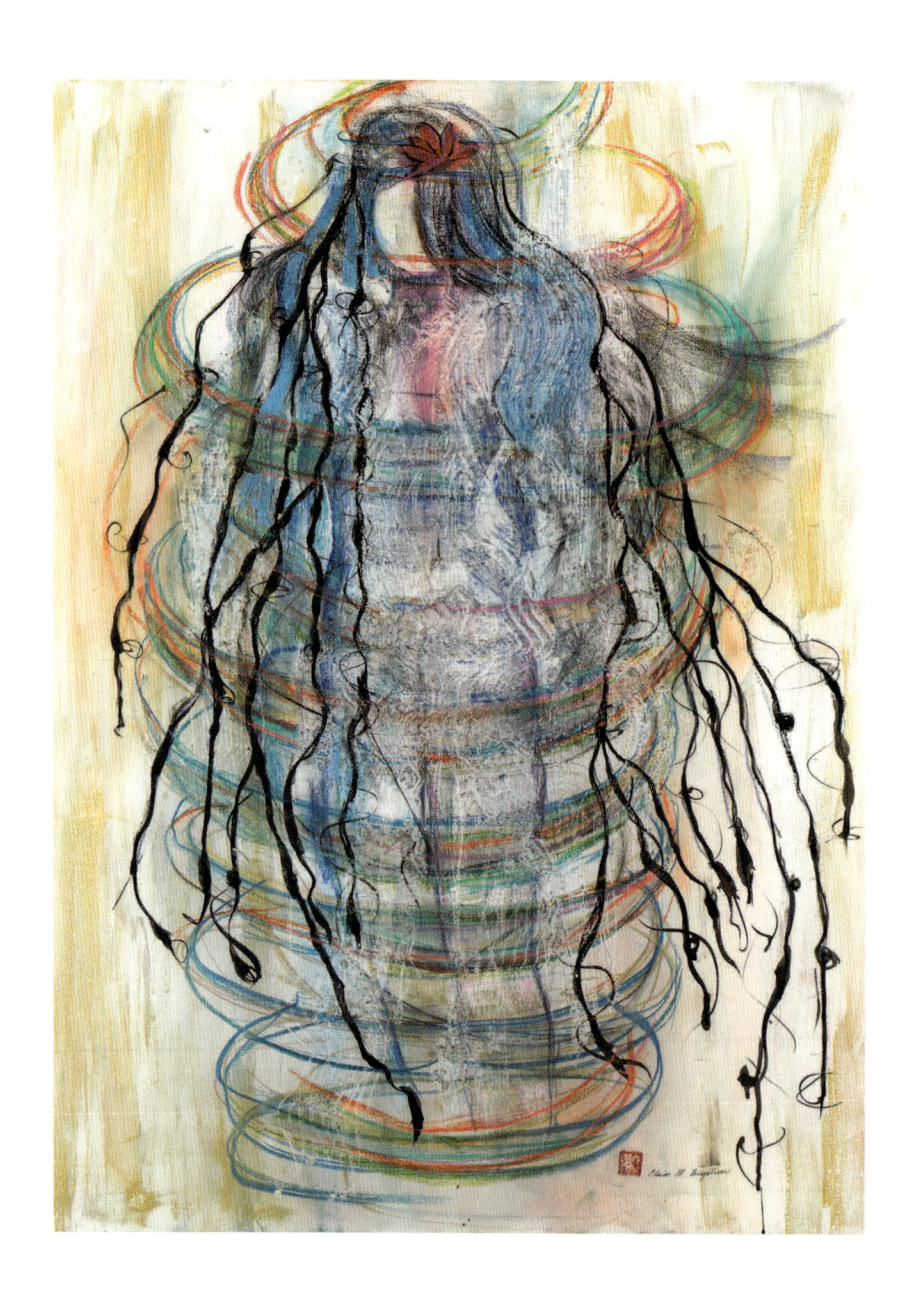

TANGLED UP • Elaine Bergstrom • *mixed media, watercolor on canvas with Sumi ink*

This series was an exploration of my insight through a spiritual journey that was unleashed, untangled, and contemplated through the influence of chakras, Kabbalah, Asian culture, and energy swirls. I pulled my ideas from traditional Chinese painting techniques, botanical illustration, and design education. The symbols are vessels of light, orbs, chakras, and the energy swirls from Kundalini meditation. (SHINE exhibition, Spring 2019)

WESTCUTTER ISLAND
Sarah Shields

i am with you
on this wind-swept field
middle of the english channel
grass so green
it could knock you down
or make you cry
clouds coming quickly
some black-gray
some wisp-white
sunlight fighting for angles
slipping in on bright blue panes of sky
why are you here with me?
it could be 1941
or 2021
damn you!
with your slivers of possibility
on the quick flashes of sunlight
in the gloom
time traveling with your understanding frown
and all-knowing eyes
"how can that cliff be so flat?" i would ask you
and you would know
or I would be happy
with your question-answer
speak to me like a 5-year-old child
then ask me a question like an insecure lover
we can fish from this island forever
i'll turn their little bodies over a fire
on the beach
until their scaly skin crackles
and we'll laugh and pull away the flesh with our fingers
careful not to choke on any bones
we can sleep in caves
with a seaweed mattress
and a driftwood headboard
i could sleep the sleep of the dead here
dreamless
with my sandy arm draped over your shoulder
there are places with this color palette that make sense
for you and me
churning changing grays
foaming, whipping whites
solid, dense blacks
opportunistic blues
and the brightest, greenest, greens chlorophyll ever overachieved.

(a) river rising • anthology of women's voices

MORNING LIGHT • Bronwen Chandler • *acrylic on canvas*

The morning sun edging over the horizon and lighting the ocean's surface is a visible interpretation of how light can ignite our souls. (SHINE exhibition, Spring 2019)

ARTIST'S DAY AT THE BEACH
Marilyn Jones

It's Wednesday, but I'm not going in to work today. I planned ahead, took the day off, and scheduled an "artist's date" for myself. I'm going to the beach! The thought of spending time at the beach on a Wednesday afternoon feels wonderfully self-indulgent. I throw my beach chair in the back of the car, pick up a smoothie for lunch, and head to the beach. It's an insanely sunny, gorgeous October afternoon. I park the car and walk the short distance to the beach, chair in one hand and smoothie in the other. I set up my chair, then I sit. I sip. I surrender.

I mentally review the instructions for what Julia Cameron calls an artist's date. Something done alone. An opportunity to nurture yourself or indulge in something you wouldn't normally do. Time to observe. To play. To create. To let your mind wander. To be totally in the moment. To shut down the usually dominant analytical, left side of the brain. To relax and allow the right side of the brain, the intuitive, creative side, to take over for awhile.

I recline my chair and slowly begin to relax, shutting down the verbal chatter in my head and allowing my senses to take over. The rhythm of the crashing waves lulls me into an even deeper state of relaxation. It's windy and I feel the cool breeze on my skin. Actually, it's more than cool. The wind is surprisingly cold for October. The jeans and long-sleeved shirt I'm wearing are not keeping me warm. Shivering, I draw my legs in close and wrap my arms around me. It's noon and, despite the cold breeze, the bright sun is directly overhead, beating down intensely on the small area of skin on my upper chest exposed by the V-neck of my shirt. Such a strange sensation—to be shivering from the cold while at the same time feeling this exposed part of my body burning hot—literally, reddening from the intensity of the noon sun.

It reminds me of autumns in the Midwest, where I lived for many years. I remember standing around bonfires at parties with the side of my body nearest the fire feeling toasty and warm and the side away from the fire feeling the sharp cold of the night air. As if back in Ohio, I smell the smoke from the fire and see the stars shining bright in the clear, dark sky. I feel the icy, cold bottle of beer in my hand. I hear the laughter and feel the closeness of good friends. When one side of my body becomes either too hot or too cold, I turn the other side towards the fire. Like the slow turning of a marshmallow on a stick over an open flame, I turn my body strategically, moving to even out my body temperature, striving to feel pleasantly warm all over, like a perfectly toasted, golden brown marshmallow.

A cloud momentarily blocks out the noon sun, and suddenly, I'm back on the beach in Jacksonville. I open my eyes and see the bright blue sky and billowing white clouds. I remember what Becky said in our writing circle last week, that artists will squint their eyes to make the color palette more apparent. So I squint my eyes, and the beach's palette of blues, grays, and whites is now obvious to me in a way I've never noticed before. Still squinting, I notice something else—lines, lines I've never noticed before. The line where the sand ends and the water begins. The line of waves moving into the shore. The straight line of the horizon, neatly dividing the ocean and the sky.

Suddenly, I'm reminded of a piece of artwork I own. It's an ocean scene, with an interesting use of lines and a blue, gray, and white palette—the same as what I see before me now.

It just so happens that I'm in the process of redoing my bedroom, and I'm painting it blue. I decide to replace the print that's over my bed with the seascape painting. The one with the blue, gray, and white palette and the pattern of lines, neither of which, until today, I had ever noticed before. No, not when my left brain was in charge.

A final sip of my smoothie and I get up to leave. I can feel the heat radiating from the patch of sunburned skin on my chest and neck. Not quite the evenly toasted marshmallow I always strive for.

—The Artist's Way Series, Fall 2015

SPEAK, BRAVE HEARTS • Margete Griffin • *screen print, wheat paste*

I am primarily a screen printer using images and words that represent the traits and actions of people. My goal is to shed light on an issue, or cause, so I can contribute my voice. My art uncensored is my best way to rise and shine. I am a translator of struggles and a beacon of encouragement. I do not have all of the answers, and do not tell people how to think, but compel them to think.
(RISE Exhibition, Fall 2018)

CLASS POEM #1
Nancy Murrey-Settle

Sitting in front of me, thirty-plus of you in rows,
poised to grow, I hope. Daring to know,
following Immanuel Kant's call to
emerge from immaturity, to think for yourself.

This world needs you. This world needs more butterflies,
more female scientists, more Maria Sibylla Merian.
I wish you godspeed, as you set sail for South America,
or, wherever your path leads.

Diderot published his Encyclopedia,
spreading enlightened ideals of his time.
May you write volume upon volume,
insights for this new century, carefully crafting
your digital mark on the fabric of our society.

We need your enthusiasm, your potential
the way you accept people for who they are,
not who you want them to be.
We need your skepticism, your voice, your vote.

Kids, the old guard mumbles, shakes its head,
wiggles its finger,
and calls you babies.
Yet I see you, waiting for your turn.

Now you are a student in a box
like Luther was a monk in a cell.
Luther turned the world on its head
and didn't lose his in the process.

You might make us right again. This is my hope—
that you will rise to the call of humankind,
seek and explore, discover and enlighten
become a present-day Copernicus,
show that being human
does not revolve around the corporate sphere.

Instead of quibbling about a point on a grade
I beseech you to squabble instead
about our freedoms, not let them slip away.
I call on you to stand before the inquisition of our day,
be present, let your voice be heard.

SOUL TO SOLE
Michelle Deluca

It started out as just a typical morning of service for Generation Works. I was assigned to the City Rescue Mission Thrift Store. I have never been a shopper of thrift stores, but on the giving end of numerous donations over the years. One brief encounter in the warehouse, an introduction from the manager, and I was transported into another world—a world that changed my perception of both shoes and myself.

Our group was taken to a back room filled with big boxes of shoes. Our assignment was to empty the shoes on the floor, sort through them, find the matching pair, and rubber band them so they could be sold.

Easy enough, right? We started and emptied out box after box, literally hundreds of shoes, onto the cement floor. There were shoes of all sizes, shapes, colors and styles: men's, women's and children's, Nike gym shoes, everyday casual shoes, slippers and boots, high-end designer shoes, and flip-flops.

As I began to touch each shoe, my mind started to wander, thinking about each person who wore them. What kind of person were they? What were their interests? Were they happy? I was picking up on their energy and wondering what it was like to walk in their shoes—what their journey was all about. Each shoe had an owner. Each person had a story, a story that should be told. I was totally transfixed in the moment.

My observation was that on one end of the spectrum, a good majority of the shoes were almost new, hardly worn, while on the other end were shoes that looked like they were chewed up by the dog, missing a heel, or just plain worn out. Then there were hundreds of shoes without a matching pair. Where did the other shoe go? To shoe heaven?

Recently, I stumbled across boxes of my own shoes. Most of them didn't fit me any longer.; yes, even my feet have grown bigger and wider as I've aged. I separated them into three piles: trash, donate to Goodwill, and the good ones to the Women's Center of Jacksonville. I am embarrassed to admit, I had three large boxes of shoes, most of them new or hardly worn designer shoes. I was happy about it, knowing they would go to good use. But I was also ashamed and humbled by this experience. What made me any different? What was my story? Are there women out there wearing my shoes, picking up on my energy?

I know I have always been one of the lucky ones. Is it just because I was born into the right family that believed in hard work and improving lives from

> *What made me any different? What was my story? Are there women out there wearing my shoes, picking up on my energy?*

generation to generation? All of those shoes I had purchased with money I worked very hard to earn. In retrospect, it was too much waste. I was into immediate gratification then. I could have used that money to help someone less fortunate.

One simple exercise, to sort shoes, and the next thing I know, all kinds of feeling and emotions began to surface.

I grew up getting my older sister's hand-me-downs. I loved them because they were hers, and she had great style. She was seven years older, about four inches shorter, and very petite. Other than that, the thought of wearing someone else's clothes or shoes was never really an option for me. My mom and my aunt were compulsive shoppers; they used to drag me and my younger brother Ricky everywhere with them, from store to store, sale to sale, looking for bargains, but always good quality. When I think back, I was the

Soul to Sole • Michelle Deluca

best-dressed kid, everything matching—not that it was important to me, but that's what moms do.

When my sister passed away, I kept some of her clothes, shoes, and purses, even though she was a little smaller than me. My aunt told me that in the Jewish religion, when someone dies, you should never wear their shoes. It is their journey, not yours. I didn't listen. I would squeeze my feet into her shoes and like history repeating itself, I had to go through every experience she shared with me, just so I could understand it.

It took a long time for me to get rid of most of her things. With time, healing and acceptance, I realized that keeping her things would not bring her back. I finally sat down and wrote a letter to her. It was time to let go of her, so her soul could soar and rest in peace. I learned to keep her spirit alive in my heart. When I pay attention, I hear her and my mother speak through me in my laughter, my tone of voice, and my mannerisms.

I am so grateful for this Generation Works experience and the reminder that service and kindness to others is more important than buying a pair of shoes I don't need. There are children who don't have any shoes. They walk barefoot not knowing any other way. There are people who don't know where their next meal is going to come from. Each person is on their own journey. Nobody in this country should be without shoes to walk their path, or a place to sleep. or a hot meal to nourish their bodies. However that is a topic for another story.

In retrospect, I feel like I touched so many different souls that day. I felt their energy, their joy, their sorrows, their love, and their peace—but I could never really know or begin to understand their journey.

After all, I am just starting to trust the process, give up control, surrender to the universe and let my own journey unravel the way it is destined to be.

—*Generation Works volunteer event, Spring 2016*

PROMPT
When has an everyday object suddenly changed the way you view the world?

MRS. CALHOUN
Lisa Goodrich

Mrs. Calhoun was an interesting character on my childhood street. Every day at 4 p.m., she watered her grass by hand with a garden hose—the same garden hose we drank from when we were running around the neighborhood catching lizards, often in teams, putting them in Maxwell House coffee cans. I still remember that wonderful scent of coffee each time we opened the can to add to our cache. Of course, we always added a handful of grass to simulate nature for the poor, trapped little guys. Not to worry, after we compared for number of lizards caught, and determined whose collection was the biggest, we released them to tell their tales of woe to their lizard friends, probably buzzing from the caffeine contact high.

Mrs. Calhoun was probably in her mid-sixties, but I'll never know for sure. We didn't talk to her, and she didn't interact with us, though we were always running in and out of her yard. The most remarkable thing about her, and the thing that made her such a memorable figure in my childhood, was that she watered her lawn in her underwear. With large, bulbous breasts, pointy in her Playtex bra, and voluminous panties (are they panties if they're voluminous?), she was just watering away, in her front yard, every day, at 4 p.m....in her underwear.

In the beginning, the sight of her momentarily stopped our hunt, but later, as months and years passed, it became commonplace, and we hardly noticed—except when a new school friend would come over and join in the hunt. Their shock would remind us that this was not typical behavior.

While we had come to accept her daily ritual, on some level I imagined that she wasn't all there, certainly. I mean, who in their right mind??!

But here I am, 52 years old, sometimes standing in my yard (albeit the backyard), in my underwear, watering my plants. They're actually my husband's briefs, crazy comfortable and with more coverage than my bathing suit, but nonetheless, underwear. I realize now, looking back, that maybe Mrs. Calhoun wasn't crazy. Maybe she was comfortable, and isn't that what's really important?

WHAT I NEED TO REMEMBER
Kelly Komatz

I need to remember all the fun days at my grandparents' home at 459 Winter Street Extension in Troy, New York, phone number 518-283-1320. I wonder who has that number now.

They lived in a one-story ranch home in the country and had the longest driveway ever. They would often have the family over for parties, pretty much for any reason. The standing ones were always Memorial Day, Grandpa's birthday (May 24), Father's Day and my birthday (often combined), July Fourth, Grandma's birthday (July 20) and Labor Day. No parties in August since we were all in Cape Cod at Hurricane Pines for that month.

In the summer, my grandfather would turn the attached garage into a party room. He had screens made that fit into the garage door so when the sun went down, or the insects were plentiful, we could continue the parties without interruption.

He also wired speakers into the garage (mind you, this was in the 1960s, early 1970s) and music could play from their stereo in the parlor (they didn't have a living room) to the garage. Oh, the songs and the singing! What joyous days.

We kids would sleep in sleeping bags on the parlor floor at night. The furniture was covered in plastic. They had a clock in there that would chime every 15 minutes. I have the clock now but, unfortunately, it is no longer able to work, even after someone fixed it. During the garage parties, we kids were not allowed into the house to use the toilet; we had to use one in the cellar. It was a portable type of toilet that people use for camping. But during those parties, we also came to learn all the old songs from my grandparents' days. And we learned to dance.

There was plenty of laughing and drinking. Being the oldest grandchild of five, I was tasked with the beer refills. Sometimes, depending upon the number of family members present, there would be a keg of beer. I learned how to pour the proper draft at the ripe old age of two years old. If it was a smaller party, then the beer was in the cellar in, of course, the beer fridge. I was schooled in the proper replacing of the beers into the fridge by rotating cold to the front, warm to the back. Another great skill to have as one grows older. I was tasked with making Grandma's gin and tonics as the day progressed. Probably something to do with the fact that I was the most reliable after a few hours into the gathering. Now, the trick here was to ensure that you put in a new lime or lemon each time the drink was made so Grandpa could keep track of just how many drinks Gracie had had.

Usually someone got in a fight with someone else, but my grandfather always seemed to manage to get everyone to bed. In the morning, most was forgotten, which I now realize was due to blackouts from being drunk. In the morning, the family usually had Bloody Marys, or, as they called them, an "eye-opener." My grandfather would say you needed to have some of the hair of the dog that bit you.

This is what I need to remember.

—*Memoir Series, Fall 2017*

ONCE UPON A TIME • Susan Gibbs Natale • *watercolor, reclaimed objects*

I am passionate about artistic intent and purpose. I love to reclaim material to create functional art. For this piece, which presents as a page from a storyboard, I employed rescued folk art, some of my early watercolors, and timeless doodle to create functional art. While it suggests a few themes, I really see this as a catalyst to a child's own imaginary travels. It offers an actual light to shine through the darkness of night.
(SHINE Exhibition, Spring 2019)

(a) river rising • anthony of women's voices

OUT OF DARKNESS • Traci Mims • *charcoal on Rives BFK paper*

I was thinking about the word "shine" as celebrating and embracing who we are as people, looking at the world and coming out of darkness—of the mind, or narrow-mindedness, and not knowing. It also represents seeing things through dark eyes in a dark face and breaking free from any type of oppression.

HE THINKS HE KNOWS ME
Cynthia Butler Jackson

He thinks he knows me, but he doesn't. It's rise and shine time! Look, he's up and in rare form. It's his slave girl game time. No, "Good morning, praise the Lord," or "How did you sleep last night?" Like magic, the fork falls on the floor, or the napkin drops, each time I reach for one.

He waits for a reaction from me. The one he is looking for is uncontrollable rage—cursing, fussing, and screaming at the top of my lungs. He loves this drama! He thinks he knows me, but he doesn't. He thinks I didn't get the message, but I did. He wants drama! I say to myself, "Maybe I can be strong and ignore him."

Holy Spirit enters briefly, whispers in my ear: "God said, the devil wants your attention. He wants your love—the heart-felt love you have. Me: "God, I told ole Satan, 'Not my daughter, you can't have her. Your only intention is to damage her and then throw her away. Cynthia is mine and you will never get her.'"

So, I sing happy songs real loud, so that it wakes the neighbors: "I Love You, Jesus, I Worship and Adore You, I Just Want to Tell You, That I Love You More Than Anything." I go down memory lane to my childhood. I begin speaking parables, like Jesus, saying things I knew would shame his childish behavior.

I finally make it through. Sit down and have my coffee with these mean-ass people, who invite themselves to the table every meal. I've got to get ready for my appointment. They follow me throughout the house, taking in every footstep I make. Waiting to see if their skillful plan to ridicule and publicly humiliate me will work. They know I have someplace to go today, a very important meeting. They do a mic check: "Can you hear her? I told you she was loud!" They walk me back-and-forth-all-over-the-house-from-room-to-room-we-go. Remember, it's a game.

On the drive to my meeting, I think to myself, "Just for this one moment, I am so relieved to get away." But then I think, "No, what if they're waiting inside?! The comrades are everywhere!"

But then I think to myself, "Just for this moment, I'm free."

When I get to the meeting, I know no one is aware of what I am really feeling inside. I hide my shame with a smile. I only want to become one of them: "A Writer, a Woman treated with respect." With no hesitation, I enter the room with grace, telling jokes and presenting a pleasant Spiritual Vibe. Concealing my true feelings—that I'm crying inside.

"Lord help me, don't let them be a group of mean people he sent to torment me!" People he tricked into joining his mockeries, his entrapments, his clever schemes to make money. I hold my head held high with grace. I don't let the group see me any different.

There are twelve women in the group, all displaying great virtues. It's like Jesus' Twelve Disciples, each bringing something valuable to the room. I'm hoping this new circle of friends will see me for the kind and gentle woman I am. Praying they will embrace me as one of them.

And I'm happy to tell you, my God was in the room, too! I could say to the group, "How blessed I am to be in the company of such strong women writers."

For in that moment, my Fear became my Honor. The tears I cried inside were Unspeakable Joy. Every prayer was answered. I have become one of the Women Writing for (a) Change in Jacksonville, Florida.

— *Flight School Discernment Circle,*
Summer 2019, Bab's Lab

LES GIRLS II • Joyce Gabiou • *mixed media*

Les Girls II is one of a pair of mixed media collages that are part of my Feminine Mystique series, an ongoing collection dedicated to all women. As an intuitive collage artist, I began by gathering black and white papers and images, then followed my intuition. (The Art of Memoir exhibition, Fall 2017)

VOICING OUR SCREAMS
Erica Saffer

The poet's face contorts; pinball machines glow. She screams over an arcade that ricochets with a mechanical retort. The lines end: she is buying milk with couch cushion change for another man's baby. I can't make out the rest, but I know exactly what she said.

Another young woman, too wise for her youth, slips into her Appalachian, remembering the taste of dollar-store canned meat. You remember everything about food when you ain't used to having it. She says the feel of a pull-tab de-fleshing a tin can lid makes her existence slither.

Then, there is me.

I'm finding a place where ideas join with minds and hearts and souls to create a community. The words once thought are now the words spoken. Awakened to a world open to the possibility that no, I'm not alone, and yes, I am home.

Then, there is me.
   There is you.
      There is us.

We're finding the words.
We're telling the stories.
We're pitching a yell.
We're yelling a voice.
We're voicing a scream.

—*Flight School School Discernment Circle, Summer 2019, Bab's Lab*

Manifesto: The Veiled Morena

Alison Fernandez • *woodblock print on fabric*

The Philippines is one of the many countries profoundly affected by colorism. We are taught to be proud of our ethnicity but not the skin color that comes with it. Those with fair skin and Eurocentric features are seen as beautiful, while those with dark skin are seen as ugly. Those with dark skin are portrayed as poor, working folk, while those with fair skin are portrayed as being wealthy enough to "stay inside." This is the result of hundreds of years of colonialism.

Whitening your skin became socially acceptable, creating a multi-billion dollar industry filled with ads of light skinned celebrities saying whiter is better, promoting whitening creams, soaps, lotions, capsules, and even injections. Even growing up in America, we are conditioned at a young age that brownness is ugly, with our parents and relatives telling us "don't stay outside too long." We grow up watching Filipino television without the accurate representation of our people. The shame that came with being brown caused us to hide behind this veil of whiteness.

TO EVERYONE:
Analyze the ways we build hierarchies rooted from discrimination and abolish them.
Question and open dialogue about normalized issues we overlook.

TO THOSE OF DARK SKIN:
Recognize the harmful imbedded messages you have learned about your brownness and fight them.
Redefine the whitewashed standards of beauty.
Love the skin you are in.

NAPAKAGANDA MO. (You are beautiful.)

DARK.

(a) river rising • anthology of women's voices

BRITTLE • Sharon Goldman • *acrylic on wood with a dried branch in her hand*

I was distressed that my neighbors were cutting their trees down due to fear of storms and pressure from money-grabbing tree-cutting services. Many were new residents to the area and didn't appreciate the beauty and importance of our lush canopy of old trees, some of which are over 100 feet tall. This is what attracted them to our neighborhood in the first place. I wanted to add a relatable visual of life in the base of the tree and emphasize that it is living and breathing, just like we are. Maybe this will give pause to someone thoughtlessly chopping down something that has been growing for years before they were alive, taking only minutes to destroy. (SHINE exhibition, Spring 2019)

SHED
Jenny Anderson

I envy the small green snake
peeking out from behind my Begonias.
Tired of her skin, she slithers out. Sloughs it off,
leaving it tangled in the leaves like a discarded coat.
One zip from eye-caps to tail and she is new.
Scales as shiny as airport shoes, she carves
through the thick St. Augustine grass. A
regal huntress, parting the tides with
ease.

I envy the patient cicada
ground-bound, larval and waiting to
push his way out of his dusty incubation.
Tree-clinging as he unwraps his iridescence
from its casing. Blazing from silence to
symphony in the course of one day.
Tymbals vibrating their eager
mating song, attracting love
on the first go-round.

But why? Why don't I have
buttons down my spine or simple snaps
to yank at when my body begs to re-emerge
as something new—when I ache to boast and shine?
Why? Why must I carry these heavy rewrites
in my cavity (this evidence of change
like anchors on my wings) when
all I really want to do is
sing?

Maybe one day you'll
see me latched barkside
to that tree. Teasing my way out
of the skin I'm in until I plunk into the dirt.
Until I slither and then fly. Shiny
and high. Leaving only
an effigy—a
hollowed out
replica
behind.

LET IT SHINE • Hope McMath • *linocut*

It might have been written as a children's song, but "This Little Light of Mine" is a powerful, beautiful song of resistance. It was also the title of a documentary about a fierce individual who stood up to oppressive systems to live her truth. So today, and every day, let your little light shine, let it shine, let it shine. (SHINE exhibition, Spring 2019)

FREE WRITE
Space for You to Create